CW00597023

EQUINOX
WARFARE

EQUINOX

EQUINOX
WARFARE

PETER HARCLERODE

First published in 2000 by Channel 4 Books, an imprint of Macmillan
Publishers Ltd, 25 Eccleston Place, London SW1W 9NF,
Basingstoke and Oxford.

Associated companies throughout the world.

www.macmillan.com

ISBN 0 7522 7215 2

Text © Peter Harclerode, 2000

The right of Peter Harclerode to be identified as the author of this work has
been asserted by him in accordance with the Copyright, Designs and
Patents Act 1988.

All rights reserved. No part of this publication may be reproduced, stored
in or introduced into a retrieval system, or transmitted, in any form, or by
any means (electronic, mechanical, photocopying, recording or otherwise)
without the prior written permission of the publisher. Any person who
does any unauthorized act in relation to this publication may be liable to
criminal prosecution and civil claims for damage.

9 7 5 3 1 2 4 6 8

A CIP catalogue record for this book is available from the British Library.

Design by Jane Coney
Typeset by Ferdinand Pageworks
Printed in Great Britain by Mackays of Chatham plc

This book is sold subject to the condition that it shall not, by way of trade
or otherwise, be lent, resold, hired out, or otherwise circulated without the
publisher's prior consent in any form of binding or cover other than that
in which it is published and without a similar condition including this
condition being imposed on the subsequent purchaser.

ACKNOWLEDGEMENTS

A number of people were kind enough to provide me with assistance during my research for this book. Mrs Lorna Arnold, former official historian at the UK Atomic Energy Research Authority and author of a number of books on nuclear energy and weapons, steered me through the unfamiliar labyrinth of nuclear technology and kindly checked my chapter on the British atomic bomb programme. Igor Kudrick of the Bellona Foundation in Oslo provided me with much information on the current process of dismantling nuclear submarines and weapons in Russia and the problems concerning security of nuclear material, while Anne Aldis of the Conflict Studies Research Centre at the Royal Military Academy Sandhurst was kind enough to bring me up to date with the current situation concerning the Strategic Rocket Forces in Russia. Duncan Lennox, editor of *Jane's Strategic Weapons Systems*, also provided me with much help on Soviet and American missile systems.

Christopher Foss, editor of *Jane's Armour and Artillery*, and weapons expert and author Ian Hogg showed great patience in answering my numerous queries on armour, artillery and other weapons systems deployed by Coalition forces during the Gulf War; and both Peter Donaldson, technology editor of *Defence Helicopter*, and Alan Warnes, editor of *Air Forces Monthly*, did likewise in assisting me on the finer points of various fixed- and rotary-wing aircraft.

Keith Atkin, editor of *Jane's Electro-Optic Systems*, provided me with much technical information and assistance regarding the various electro-optic and laser systems at present under development; while Bob Kemp, marketing communications manager at BAe Systems Avionics Group, provided me with data on the defensive infra-red counter-measures and thermal imager infra-red airborne laser designation systems currently being manufactured by his company and others.

I would like to express my sincere thanks to them all.

Finally, I am most grateful to the following producers who were kind enough to supply me with post-production scripts and research material originally used in the production of the documentaries on which this book is based: Andy Patterson and Patrick Forbes of Oxford Films & Television Company for 'A Very British Bomb'; William Woollard of Inca Films for 'Dismantling the Bomb' and 'After Desert Storm'; and David Dugan of Windfall Films for 'Russian Roulette' and 'Dawn of the Death Ray'.

PRODUCTION CREDITS

A Very British Bomb
accompanies the *Equinox* programme of the same name made
by Oxford Films & Television Company for Channel 4.
First broadcast: 15 September 1997

Dismantling the Bomb
accompanies the *Equinox* programme of the same name made
by Inca Limited for Channel 4.
First broadcast: 20 June 1996

Russian Roulette
accompanies the *Equinox* programme of the same name made
by Windfall Films for Channel 4.
First broadcast: 14 July 1998

After Desert Storm
accompanies the *Equinox* programme of the same name made
by Inca Limited for Channel 4.
First broadcast: 16 January 1993

Dawn of the Death Ray
accompanies the *Equinox* programme of the same name made
by Windfall Films for TLC and first broadcast in the USA.
First broadcast on Channel 4: 4 August 1998

CONTENTS

INTRODUCTION

From virtually the very beginning of his existence, man has employed weapons as a means of attack or defence. During the Stone Age, the humble stone was probably the first object pressed into use as a club and then as a thrown missile, followed by pieces of wood also utilized as clubs and ultimately fashioned into crude spears. The discovery of flint and the exploitation of bones enabled crude axe- and spearheads or knife blades to be fashioned. At the same time, the bow and sling were invented for the launching of shortened spears (which became arrows) and stones. Around 3500 BC saw the development of smelting, a process put to good effect by the Sumerians of Mesopotamia who discovered bronze – the first metal from which effective weapons could be fashioned. In around 1700 BC Egypt was invaded by the Hyksos, who were armed with bronze weapons and bows, and rode into battle in bronze chariots. In addition, they wore armour fashioned from leather with bronze plates attached to protect the vital parts of the body.

The first professional army was formed by Assyria in 1250 BC; it comprised chariot-mounted troops and infantry armed with weapons manufactured from iron. During the war between Persia and Greece of 490 to 479 BC, the disciplined and well-trained Greek hoplite, equipped with helmet and breastplate, a large round shield, short sword and spear, proved more than a match for the Persians. The Greeks developed the use of the phalanx, a tight formation eight men deep, with each man's shield covering the exposed right side of the man to his left. A similar system was subsequently used by the Romans until 390 BC when they introduced the legion, a unit numbering up to 6,000 men. Each legionary was equipped with helmet, armour and shield, and armed with a short stabbing sword and two *pila* (throwing spears). By this time artillery in the form of siege engines had become well developed, for example the ballista, a large mechanical bow firing a long javelin at ranges up to 500 metres, and catapults that hurled heavy rocks. Originally invented by the Sumerians, siege engines were developed further by the Assyrians and ultimately the Romans.

In western Europe, the collapse of the Roman Empire in the fifth century AD was followed by the Dark Ages, which saw a decline in military proficiency. Standing armies comprised poorly trained levies centred round small bodies of professional troops retained by the rulers who reigned following the departure of the Romans and their legions. During this period, the emphasis in weaponry turned to heavy armour, long swords, battleaxes and maces. In about AD 800 heavy cavalry came into vogue and for the following 500 years reigned supreme on the battlefield. The arrival of the longbow, however, spelt the end for heavily armoured knights as was shown at the Battle of Crécy in 1346 when English longbowmen slaughtered over 1,500 French heavy cavalry as well as some 10,000 foot-soldiers and lightly armed levies.

The advent of gunpowder resulted in the development of artillery and, by the middle of the fifteenth century, most armies in Europe were equipped with some form of cannon. Manufactured in iron with short barrels, they were intended for siege warfare and fired solid round balls of stone designed to batter down the walls of castles or defensive emplacements. Handguns had made their first appearance in the middle of the fourteenth century; heavy and cumbersome, they were little more than miniature cannon and possessed little accuracy. The middle of the fifteenth century, however, saw the arrival of the matchlock arquebus, a heavy smoothbore weapon fired from the shoulder with the barrel of the weapon supported by a rest.

The next two centuries saw a number of further developments, especially in the field of hand-held and shoulder-fired weapons, with the arrival of the wheel-lock and flint-lock. Artillery also saw vast improvements and by 1600 had been standardized into four types: culverins, for long range up to 6,460 metres (21,195 feet); cannons, capable of firing a 40-kilogram (90-pound) ball up to some 3,690 metres (12,100 feet); pedreros, which could fire a 27-kilogram (60-pound) projectile up to 1,846 metres (6,055 feet); and mortars, which could send a 90-kilogram (200-pound) shell up to 2,300 metres (7,545 feet) in a high trajectory.

The eighteenth century saw little in the way of radical changes in weapons, with muzzle-loading artillery and small arms continuing in service well into the next century. One of the most significant developments during that period was the introduction into military use of the rifled barrel, which had hitherto been a feature of sporting weapons. At that time the standard military weapon was the smoothbore musket, which was not a particularly accurate weapon at ranges over 50 metres (165 feet). Rifles were, however, capable of producing accurate fire at ranges of between 200 and

300 metres (655 and 985 feet) and first proved their worth during the American War of Independence, when American irregulars used them with great effect against the British. The latter learned the lesson well and in about 1800 introduced the Baker rifle, which was used by the British Army's rifle regiments during the Napoleonic Wars, being replaced by the Brunswick rifle in 1837.

The first half of the nineteenth century saw a number of major advances, including the invention of the first breech-loading weapons. Others included the development of the revolver by American Samuel Colt in the late 1830s, and the first machine-gun, invented by Richard Gatling, which saw service during the American Civil War. The last thirty years of the century saw major advances in the design of automatic weapons, which would have a major impact on military strategy and tactics.

Without doubt, the twentieth century was the most destructive and violent in the history of warfare, featuring two world wars and a large number of regional conflicts. It also saw the development of armaments and weapons systems that would have far-reaching and long-lasting ramifications for almost the entire world, in particular nuclear weaponry which for nearly fifty years posed the threat of mutual destruction by the superpowers.

The First World War was essentially a static conflict fought in the trenches and resulting in huge loss of life on both sides. Artillery was used extensively in support of mass infantry attacks but frequently proved ineffective against well-dug-in troops who, once a barrage had been lifted, opened fire with large numbers of machine-guns. They would cause extensive casualties among attacking troops, whose forays were frequently held up by barbed wire which had also been little affected by shellfire. Among newly developed weapons that made their appearances during the four years of the war were flame throwers, poison gas and tanks. The latter were used first by the British in September 1916. However, at the end of the Battle of the Somme they suffered heavy losses through mechanical breakdown and inexperienced tank crews. The Germans were quick to react to this new threat, developing the first generation of anti-tank weapons.

The First World War was also notable for the introduction of aircraft in a military role. Initially used primarily for reconnaissance and observation, these first unarmed models were equipped with early-generation radios via which they transmitted target co-ordinates in Morse code to the artillery, who thereafter acted on the information. In due course fighters were also developed, seeing extensive service on both sides.

The 1920s and 1930s saw further developments in the field of armour, including the design and development of tanks with rotating turrets containing the main armament. Although Britain, the United States, France, Italy and Russia carried out much experimentation with armoured and mechanized formations, it was the Germans who developed the strategy of *blitzkrieg* and used it with such devastating success during the invasion of Poland in 1939 and that of Belgium, Holland and France in 1940. The ensuing five years of conflict saw considerable research and development of weaponry on both sides, particularly in the areas of armoured fighting vehicles, anti-tank weapons and armour-piercing ammunition.

The Second World War was also notable for the birth of the first strategic weapons in the form of *Vergeltungswaffen* (reprisal weapons), better known as V-weapons, developed by Germany. From June 1944 to March 1945 Britain was subjected to over 8,000 attacks by V1 pilotless flying bombs, the forerunner of today's cruise missile, which were launched from the Pas de Calais on the coast of northern France and from Holland. Popularly known as the 'doodle-bug'. From September 1944 onwards, it was joined by the even more terrifying V2 missile which, although inaccurate, could reach target areas up to about 320 kilometres (200 miles). Travelling faster than the speed of sound, it would arrive completely unheralded until announcing its presence with a massive explosion. The use of V-weapons was indiscriminate. They were aimed at cities and other densely populated areas, and were designed to instil terror into the populations of London and southern England.

Meanwhile, Britain and America were aware of Germany's and Japan's efforts to develop nuclear weapons and thus were determined to pre-empt them by producing their own. The United States, with British assistance, succeeded in winning the race and the dropping of two atomic bombs on Hiroshima and Nagasaki in 1945 hastened the subsequent surrender of Japan.

However, as described in 'A Very British Bomb', after the end of the war Britain discovered that the United States no longer wished to continue the close wartime collaboration and was thus forced to establish its own nuclear weapons programme. Despite major problems and opposition from the United States, it succeeded in doing so and carried out its first test of an atomic bomb in October 1952. Meanwhile, however, treachery on the part of British and American scientists had permitted the Russians to develop their own atomic bomb, which was exploded in August

1949. Development of thermonuclear weapons by the United States, Britain and the Soviet Union swiftly ensued and the years following the end of the Second World War and the beginning of the Cold War saw the start of the nuclear arms race between the superpowers.

Massive resources were devoted by the United States and the Soviet Union to the development of strategic nuclear weapons and the systems to deliver them. Initially, the Soviets relied on long-range heavy bombers for delivery of nuclear weapons, but by the end of the 1950s had also developed intermediate range ballistic missiles (IRBMs). Development of second-generation weapons was by then at an advanced stage and in 1963 intercontinental ballistic missiles (ICBMs), such as the SS-8 Sasin, were deployed. These were followed by third-generation weapons and in the late 1960s by the development of the first Soviet multiple warhead systems known as multiple re-entry vehicles (MRVs). Equipped with an MRV system, the SS-9 Scarp was capable of delivering three warheads, all of which would either attack the same target, to maximize the chance of destroying it, or three individual targets within an area known as the missile's 'footprint'.

In addition to land-based ICBMs, the Soviets also developed submarine-launched ballistic missiles (SLBMs). Development of strategic ballistic missile submarines (SSBNs) followed.

By the end of the 1960s, the United States had also developed a formidable arsenal of strategic nuclear weapons. Like the Soviet Union, during the late 1940s and early 1950s it had developed a long-range bomber, the B-52 Stratofortress, for the aerial delivery of nuclear weapons; but during the 1960s it concentrated on the development of

ICBMs. First among these were the Atlas and the Titan I. Phased out in the mid-1960s, Titan I was followed by the Titan II, a much larger missile with a 9-megaton warhead, which remained the principal US ICBM until the arrival of the Minuteman I. The latter was soon replaced in the late 1960s by Minuteman II, which had a range of 13,000 kilometres (8,000 miles) and a 1.2-megaton warhead equipped with electronic jamming devices and other systems designed to enable it to penetrate Soviet radar-controlled anti-ballistic missile systems. A further enhanced version, Minuteman III, entered service between 1970 and 1975, the first US missile to be equipped with a multiple independently targeted re-entry vehicle (MIRV) system comprising three MIRVs, each equipped with a 170-kiloton warhead.

The United States also developed SLBMs, the first being the Polaris A-1 which became operational in 1960. This was followed two years later by the A2 model and eventually the A3, the latter being the first American SLBM to be equipped with MIRVs. All three models of Polaris were deployed aboard Benjamin Franklin and Lafayette Class SSBNs which at the end of the 1960s were converted to carry a new SLBM: the Poseidon C3.

Both the United States and the Soviet Union also developed tactical nuclear weapons for delivery on to the battlefield by short and intermediate range ballistic missiles fired from mobile launchers. Among those in the American inventory were the MGR-1 Honest John and the MGM-52 Lance battlefield missiles. The latter, which entered service in 1971 to replace the Honest John, could be fitted with a variety of warheads, ranging from one to 100 kilotons. A more advanced weapon was the MGM-31 Pershing 1a IRBM which, with a maximum range of 740 kilometres (460 miles) and a range of warheads of up to 400 kilotons, entered service in 1962. It was replaced in 1984 by the Pershing II which, fitted with a manoeuvring warhead (MaRV), was an exceptionally accurate weapon with a range of 1,800 kilometres (1,120 miles).

The Soviet Union meanwhile produced the FROG-7 unguided battlefield rocket and the SS-1C Scud B SRBM, both entering service in 1965. In 1969 the SS-12 Scaleboard SRBM also became operational. In 1978 the SS-21 Spider entered service as a replacement for the FROG-7. Mounted on an armoured 6 × 6 amphibious transporter/launch vehicle, it had a range of 120 kilometres (75 miles) and carried a 100-kiloton warhead. In 1985, a replacement for the Scud appeared in the form of the SS-23 Scarab.

By the beginning of the 1970s, the Soviet Union had achieved numerical superiority over the United States in terms of operational ICBMs. During the following decade it proceeded to develop further IRBMs and ICBMs with increasing range and enhanced warhead capabilities. In 1975 the first MIRV-equipped ICBMs were deployed, prominent among them being the SS-18 Satan. In addition the SS-20 IRBM was developed and deployed in early 1976. Mounted on a tracked chassis, it could be equipped with a 1.5-megaton warhead and had a range of 2,750 kilometres (1,700 miles). The SS-20 caused considerable concern to the United States and its allies as it had the capability, depending on its deployment location within the Soviet Union, of hitting targets throughout the whole of western Europe and the Middle East.

The Soviets also developed fourth-generation SLBMs which came into service during the 1970s and were operational aboard Delta Class SSBNs. Late 1976 saw the arrival of the SS-N-18 Model 1 which, with a range of 6,500 kilometres (4,000 miles), was the first Soviet SLBM to be equipped with a MIRV warhead system. The most startling development, however, was the Typhoon SSBN which entered operational service in 1983. The largest underwater vessel ever constructed and powered by four pressurized water-cooled nuclear reactors, it was designed to operate within the Arctic Circle from which it would launch its twenty SLBMs against targets throughout the continental United States.

The United States had meanwhile also developed a new SLBM, and in 1979 deployed the Trident I C4 aboard eight Benjamin Franklin and Lafayette SSBNs converted to carry it. In 1989 an enhanced version, the Trident II D5, came into service and was deployed on new Ohio Class SSBNs designed to carry the new missile, which has a range of 7,400 to 11,100 kilometres (4,560 to 6,900 miles) and is equipped with between eight and fourteen MIRVs, each with a 375-kiloton warhead.

By the late 1960s, it had become apparent that neither the United States nor the Soviet Union could hope to win a nuclear conflict as both had the capability to inflict an equal amount of destruction on the other. Thus 1969 had seen the start of the Strategic Arms Limitation Talks (SALT), the aim of which was to halt the strategic nuclear arms race. Further progress on nuclear disarmament began in 1982 with the Strategic Arms Reductions Talks (START), which culminated in 1991 with the START I treaty.

In 1980 the United States and the Soviet Union began negotiations over the elimination of IRBMs, which were defined as weapons having ranges of 1,000 to 5,500 kilometres (620 to 3,400 miles). This resulted in the signing of the Intermediate-Range Nuclear Forces (INF) Treaty of 1987, which also covered SRBMs with ranges of 500 to 1,000 kilometres (300 to 620 miles) and called for the progressive dismantling over a period of three years of a total of 2,619 missiles, two-thirds of which were Soviet.

December 1991 saw the dissolution of the Soviet Union and its replacement by fifteen independent states of which four – Russia, Ukraine, Belarussia and Kazakhstan – still retained strategic and tactical nuclear weapons within their respective territories. In January 1993 the United States and Russia signed an informal agreement, START II, under which ICBMs with MIRV warheads would be destroyed and numbers of strategic warheads limited to between 3,000 and 3,500 by the end of the year 2007. In addition, a limit of 1,700 to 1,750 was placed on warheads deployed on SLBMs. Ratification of the treaty by the US Senate took place in January 1996 but it would not be until April 2000 that the Russian Duma would do likewise.

As recounted in 'Dismantling the Bomb', destruction of nuclear weapons in the United States began in 1991 at a special facility formerly used for the servicing and maintenance of missiles and bombs. The situation was, however, very different in the four former Soviet states, which were virtually bankrupt and unable to fund their respective dismantlement programmes. In early 1991 informal approaches were made to the United States for assistance, and these ultimately led to the establishment of the Co-operative Threat Reduction (CTR) Program, also known as the Nunn–Lugar Program after the two US senators who conceived it. Since then, the United States has committed substantial financial and technical assistance to Ukraine, Belarussia and Kazakhstan in becoming nuclear-free states, and to Russia in helping to overcome the problems of reducing its nuclear weapons arsenal.

Such is the size of Russia's nuclear stockpile, however, and the poor conditions under which much of it is stored, that its security poses a major problem. The United States, well aware of the risk of nuclear material falling into the hands of countries keen to develop their own nuclear weapons, has thus provided funds under the auspices of the CTR Program to improve security measures and finance the construction of special storage facilities. As told in 'Russian Roulette', however, a number of miniaturized tactical nuclear weapons, popularly referred to as 'suitcase bombs' because of the briefcases in which they were installed, were found to be missing from Russian arsenals and their whereabouts have as yet not been confirmed.

At the beginning of the last century, standard infantry weapons in the majority of armies comprised bolt-action rifles and water-cooled machine-guns, while cavalry were mounted on horses and equipped with swords, lances and carbines. Artillery provided support with shrapnel fired by field guns and howitzers at ranges up to 9,150 metres (29,740 feet). Wireless was non-existent and communication was by heliograph, semaphore flags and signal lamp. Aircraft had not been invented and thus air warfare was a dimension yet to be added to the battlefield.

Ninety years later the picture was very different when, during the Gulf War of 1991, Coalition forces in Saudi Arabia engaged those of Iraq a few months after the latter's invasion of Kuwait. As described in 'After Desert Storm', hostilities opened with US Army helicopter gunships destroying two key radars located near the Iraqi/Saudi border, thereby allowing a stream of aircraft to pour through the gap created in Iraqi air defences. Among them were F-117A Stealth fighters, which were invisible to the air defence radars and surface-to-air missile batteries seeking vainly to shoot them down. Meanwhile, warships and nuclear-powered submarines in the Persian Gulf launched salvoes of Tomahawk cruise missiles which subsequently navigated themselves over the 1,000 kilometres (600 miles) of terrain to the Iraqi capital of Baghdad, where they unerringly sought out their respective targets and destroyed them.

During the following ground war, artillery – comprising guns and multi-launch rocket systems, all directed by computerized target data and fire control computers – pounded Iraqi troops at ranges of between 20 and 30 kilometres (12 to 18 miles). When Coalition forces advanced into Kuwait the infantry, armed with self-loading rifles and automatic weapons that could be equipped with night-vision devices enabling them to see and engage the enemy in the dark, were transported into battle in armoured vehicles or by helicopter. They had their own defence against enemy armour in the form of shoulder-fired rockets or medium-range anti-tank guided weapons. In constant radio communication with members of their unit and those of others, they were able to navigate through the most featureless of terrain courtesy of satellite navigation systems. They were supported by main battle tanks featuring computerized fire control systems for their 120-mm guns and equipped with steel-ceramic composite armour providing very high levels of ballistic protection. Meanwhile, helicopter gunships engaged Iraqi armour and infantry with guided missiles, rockets and chain guns, destroying them in large numbers. In the sky above, E-3 Sentry AWACS and E-8 JSTARS aircraft provided information on targets and directed air and ground attacks against them.

Such were the scenes that took place eleven years ago. But what of warfare in the future? Despite the major reduction in the threat of global nuclear conflict between the United States and Russia, the risk of nuclear proliferation has remained, with countries such as Iran, Iraq and North Korea seeking to develop their own nuclear weapons. These and others currently possess short- and medium-range ballistic missiles with ranges up to 3,000 kilometres (1,860 miles) and capable of carrying high explosive or chemical agent warheads.

Furthermore, China possesses approximately twenty CSS-4 ICBMs, all of which are capable of reaching the United States, and is known to be developing two mobile ICBMs. The first of these, designated the DF-31, was tested in August 1999 and intelligence sources judge it will have a range of approximately 8,000 kilometres (5,000 miles). The second missile to be tested between 2000 and 2002 and to possess a longer range. A US National Intelligence Council report, published in September 1999, stated that by 2015 China is anticipated to have tens of ICBMs targeted against the United States.

In order to provide defence against these and similar weapons, a number of counter-measures are currently under development. One such system, mounted in a large aircraft and comprising a high-energy chemical laser capable of emitting massive power, is designed to engage and destroy launched Theatre Ballistic Missiles (TBMs) as they break through the clouds near the edge of the Earth's atmosphere. Further anti-ballistic defence will be provided at even greater altitudes by a US space-based system scheduled to be operational by the year 2010. Comprising six high-energy lasers mounted on satellites, its role will be to engage ICBMs launched anywhere on the Earth's surface.

Meanwhile, it seems that lasers will play an increasing part in conventional warfare, primarily in a defensive role. As described in 'Dawn of the Death Ray', an example of this is a ground-based system, currently nearing completion of development, which is designed to provide defence against short-range battlefield rockets of the Russian 122-mm Katyusha type. Two other systems, fitted to aircraft and armoured vehicles respectively, have been produced to blind the homing heads of infra-red guided missiles launched at them. Further research is currently being conducted into the development of lasers for use as attack weapons for precision strikes against targets with minimum collateral damage to personnel and surrounding areas. It thus appears that they may well become the weapons of the future.

In over 2,000 years of history, man has devoted much of his ingenuity to the development and production of increasingly deadly and destructive weapons, the most dreadful being nuclear weapons capable of devastating entire nations. Despite the partial dismantling of stockpiles of nuclear weapons held by the United States and Russia and the consequent lowering of the risk of global nuclear conflagration, the threat of conflict is still present in several parts of the globe. It seems that man is unlikely ever to learn from his mistakes and all too easily forgets the lessons of the past. Perhaps it would be as well to remember the words written in 1965 by an eminent military historian, the late Brigadier Peter Young, which are still very relevant thirty-five years later: 'We live in a technological age. But it is an age in which people whose interests are opposed still strive to solve their problems by force, though their methods may be those of the economist, the politician and the diplomat. Perhaps two world wars have bred a brand of statesman capable of keeping the lid on Hell. It does not seem likely, for we are not especially skilful in selecting our masters. Let us therefore remember the words of Santayana: "He who forgets his history is condemned to relive it."'

A VERY
BRITISH BOMB

On 6 August 1945 a United States Army Air Force B-29 bomber dropped an atomic bomb over the Japanese city of Hiroshima; three days later, on 9 August, another was dropped over Nagasaki. Such was the massive loss of life and devastation that five days later, on 14 August, Japan surrendered unconditionally.

The United States had won the race to develop an atomic weapon and in so doing had brought the Second World War, which had lasted almost six years, to a conclusion. The Americans could not have done so, however, without the powerful impetus of Britain and vital input from British scientists, who had been the first to demonstrate that an atomic bomb was possible. A small group of the latter later played crucial roles in the highly secret Manhattan Project, the codename of the American atomic weapon development programme.

Britain had been involved in nuclear research since before 1940, and had been very much in the lead during that period. It was a British scientist, Professor James Chadwick, who had discovered the neutron in 1932 (and was awarded a Nobel prize for the discovery in 1935). In late 1938, in Berlin, Otto Hahn and Fritz Strassmann discovered the phenomenon of nuclear fission in uraniam bombarded by slow neutrons. The full import of it was not understood, however, until shortly afterwards when Lise Meitner and her nephew, Otto Frisch, both refugees from Nazi persecution, interpreted this phenomenon as nuclear fission (a term borrowed from biology by Frisch). The practical possibility of a fast chain reaction resulting in an atomic bomb was recognized in Britain in 1940 by Frisch and Professor Rudolf Peierls, the latter also a refugee from Nazi Germany. In February that year, they produced a short but convincing memorandum stating that if uranium-235, which comprises 0.7 per cent of natural uranium, could be separated from the rest of the material, it would be possible to produce a bomb using only a small amount. Furthermore, although separation would be difficult, uranium-235 had the potential to make a very powerful weapon. Up to that time, it had been calculated that the amount needed to bring about an explosive reaction was impracticably large to produce, and would mean a bomb too large to be carried by any aircraft.

Peierls and Frisch foresaw the long-term hazards of radiation and fall-out, and concluded their three-page memorandum by stating that they thought it likely that the Allies would never wish to develop such a bomb. It was intrinsically a weapon of mass destruction that would inevitably cause much civilian death and suffering. The sole reason for their bringing this to the attention of the government was their fear that Germany might already be working on the development of atomic weapons, and their conviction that the only effective deterrent would be for the Allies to possess their own. The Germans were indeed carrying out nuclear research for military purposes and during 1940 the British received warnings from France and other sources to that effect.

The memorandum had the desired effect. It soon reached the highest levels of government where it resulted in the establishment of the high-powered committee, code-named MAUD, which in July 1941 produced two detailed reports. The first examined the principle of an atomic weapon, method of fusing, probable effect, the preparation of material and the resources, including time and cost, that would be required to produce a uranium bomb. It stated that 25 pounds (over 11 kilograms) of uranium-235 would be needed for an explosive yield of 1.8 kilotons, equivalent to 1,800 tons of TNT. The second report examined how uranium could be used to fuel a reactor that could be used not only as a source of power but also to produce a new fissile material, 'Element 94', later named plutonium. Plutonium-239 would be an even better explosive than uranium-235.

Copies of both reports were despatched to the United States where the scientific establishment, which at that time was concentrating solely on research into nuclear fission for peaceful purposes, was slow on the uptake. It should be remembered that at this point the Americans were not participants in the war against Germany, and thus there was no incentive for research for military purposes. Meanwhile, unknown to all those involved, copies also found their way to Moscow courtesy of a Soviet agent inside the British government. Although the culprit was never officially identified, the finger of suspicion would later be pointed at John Cairncross, a young civil servant who at the time of the MAUD report was working in the private office of Lord Hankey, the cabinet minister responsible for scientific matters.

On the strength of these reports, the British government decided to proceed with research and development of an atomic bomb. Indeed, the decision was taken at the highest level, by the Prime Minister, Winston Churchill, himself, and the level of secrecy was such that not even the War Cabinet was consulted about it. Responsibility for the project was given to the Department of Scientific and Industrial Research, which in the autumn of 1941 formed the Directorate of Tube Alloys. This was responsible for overseeing research carried out by a number of establishments including the Cavendish and Clarendon laboratories at Cambridge and Oxford respectively, as well as laboratories at the universities of Bristol, Birmingham and Liverpool.

By the latter part of 1941, the British were ahead of the United States in uranium research and thus had much to offer a combined Anglo–American project. But when approached by the Americans to pool resources, they responded coolly, citing fears over security and making it apparent that they wanted to restrict collaboration to exchanges of information. The situation changed dramatically, however, on 7 December 1941 when Japanese aircraft attacked ships of the US Navy's Pacific Fleet at its base at Pearl Harbor, Hawaii, sinking four battleships, damaging a number of other vessels and destroying 180 aircraft. US casualties totalled over 3,400, of whom more than 2,300 were killed. On the following day the United States declared war on Japan and, within days, on Germany and Italy.

Now that they were combatants, the Americans lost no time in beginning work on their own atomic weapon programme. Swiftly allocating considerable resources to it, they pushed ahead independently and such was the speed of their progress that by June 1942 they had surged ahead of the British. By this time the latter had changed their minds and were seeking close collaboration on the lines previously proposed by the Americans, who now, however, no longer regarded British input as essential to their programme. When a team of scientists, led by the head of the Tube Alloys directorate, Wallace Akers, visited the United States early in 1942, they found that the Americans were already overtaking them in development of processes for producing fissile material. Furthermore, they discovered that uranium-235 was no longer the material most likely to be used in nuclear weapons, plutonium by then being the Americans' first choice.

The increasing American lead inevitably resulted in a corresponding reduction in British bargaining power with regard to Anglo–American collaboration, and by the late summer of 1942 it became apparent that the likelihood of integrating British and American research efforts was fading fast. Moreover, the free exchange of information, maintained since July 1941, appeared to be coming to an end. Among those heading the Manhattan Project, including its chief General Leslie Groves, the attitude was that the British were asking for access to technology to which they had contributed little or nothing. Furthermore, doubts were being expressed among such quarters as to whether Britain should be allowed to possess nuclear weapons after the war. The situation was not helped by the fact that in September 1941 Britain had, with the knowledge of the Americans, signed an agreement with Russia for the exchange of scientific information, albeit restricted to a list of subjects approved by the United States. When President Franklin D. Roosevelt, who had previously been unaware of the agreement, was apprised of it, he endorsed proposals for restrictions being placed on exchange of information on atomic energy between the United States and Britain.

In mid-January 1943, while attending a conference with Roosevelt in Casablanca, Winston Churchill raised the subject of Anglo–American collaboration with the President's personal aide, Harry Hopkins, who assured him that the situation would be rectified by Roosevelt on his return to the United States. Nothing happened, however, and repeated communications from Churchill to Hopkins on the subject were either fobbed off or ignored.

The period of January to April 1943 saw a virtual cessation of communication between the British and American scientific establishments as they waited for the two leaders to resolve the matter. In Britain morale was very low as it became apparent that the Americans were no longer interested in collaboration. Despite the formidable cost of some 69.5 million pounds and the resources required, including 20,000 men and 500,000 tons of steel, serious consideration began to be given to the idea of Britain going it alone in building diffusion and heavy-water plants and a reactor, with the ultimate aim of producing a British bomb.

In May 1943, however, the Americans gained the monopoly of the supply of uranium and heavy water from Canada. Discovered in the early 1930s, heavy water (D_2O), also known as deuterium oxide, is used as a moderator to slow down fast-moving neutrons in order to increase their chances of hitting a nucleus and thus maintain the process of a controlled chain reaction. Later that month, Roosevelt and Churchill met again in Washington for the Trident Conference to determine future operations against Germany and Japan following victory in North Africa. The subject of Tube Alloys collaboration was raised again by Churchill and the President agreed to a resumption of exchange of information, while also concurring that the development of nuclear weapons should be a joint project. Once again, however, nothing happened.

In July the situation improved with a visit to London by Dr Vannevar Bush, chairman of the National Defense Research Committee, and the US Secretary of State for War, Henry L. Stimson. During a meeting with Stimson, Churchill succeeded in ironing out difficulties and misunderstandings relating to post-war concerns about commercial exploitation of nuclear research. It was made clear to Stimson that the British government had never attached any importance to industrial exploitation. At the same time, the Americans revealed that serious offence had been caused by the British bypassing those heading the Manhattan Project and appealing direct to President Roosevelt. The upshot of the meetings during this visit was that the obstacles to the resumption of Anglo–American collaboration were removed and a draft agreement produced. It later transpired that while Bush and Stimson were in London, Roosevelt had decided, on the advice of Harry Hopkins, to honour the undertakings he had made previously to Churchill. The President had cabled Bush in London, instructing him to reinstate full exchange of information with the British.

In August 1943 Churchill and Roosevelt met in Quebec for a conference codenamed Quadrant, at which future plans for the invasion of France and operations in the Pacific and south-east Asia were laid. On 19 August the Quebec Agreement, partly based on the draft agreement produced by the British in July, was signed by the two leaders, laying the foundations for Anglo–American collaboration in atomic weapon development for the rest of the war and ostensibly thereafter.

Four months later, in mid-December 1943, the first of a contingent of some forty British scientists left England for the United States. They were led by Professor James Chadwick, who subsequently established a close relationship with General Leslie Groves, the chief of the Manhattan Project, despite the American's reputation for being an anglophobe. Among the contingent's other members were Professor Rudolf Peierls, who later became head of the Manhattan Project's theoretical physics division; a physicist, Dr Klaus Fuchs who, like Peierls, with whom he had worked at the University of Birmingham, had fled to Britain from Nazi Germany; and William Penney, a young professor of mathematical physics. Twenty of the contingent subsequently went to Los Alamos, the American nuclear weapons laboratory located 96 kilometres (60 miles) north of Albuquerque in the mountains of New Mexico. The remainder were dispersed among other parts of the project elsewhere – with the exception of Hanford in Washington State, the site of the production reactor, from which they were excluded. While the British group was small, it was of extremely high quality and proceeded to make a disproportionate contribution to the Manhattan Project.

On 19 September 1944 Winston Churchill and President Roosevelt signed the Hyde Park Agreement, so-called because it was the name of the President's home in New York State. In this, the two countries agreed that knowledge of nuclear weapons research should be restricted to Britain and the United States, and that once a weapon had been developed it might after 'mature consideration' be used against the Japanese who should be warned that such bombing would be repeated until they surrendered. The deal also stated: 'Full collaboration between the United States and the

British government in developing tube alloys for military and commercial purposes should continue after the defeat of Japan unless and until terminated by joint agreement.'

In July 1945, however, a general election took place in Britain and the Labour government of Clement Attlee was elected to office. Attlee, despite having been Deputy Prime Minister during the war, now became fully aware for the first time of Britain's involvement in nuclear weapon research. In October, at a meeting at ShellMex House in London, the decision was taken by a small group of senior ministers within the new government to establish the Atomic Energy Research Establishment (AERE), which would have a wide-ranging brief into all aspects of nuclear research.

After Japan's surrender, and the end of the war, Britain naturally expected to continue in its nuclear partnership with the United States, under the terms of the Quebec Agreement and the Hyde Park Agreement, and at the beginning of 1947 an approach was made to the Americans for technical assistance in constructing a nuclear reactor. The British, however, received a rude shock when it was made clear to them that there was to be no further collaboration.

In May 1946 the United States had passed the Atomic Energy Act, commonly known as the McMahon Act (as it had been sponsored by Senator Brian McMahon), which established the US Atomic Energy Commission and imposed a mantle of secrecy over all aspects of nuclear energy, backed up by draconian laws banning the divulging of information of any sort relating to the subject. Furthermore, it declared that there would be no sharing of information about nuclear technology with any other nation. Part of the blame for the inclusion of Britain within the terms of the McMahon Act can be laid at the door of the tight secrecy surrounding the Quebec Agreement of August 1943 and the Hyde Park Agreement of September 1944, of which Congress had no knowledge. Senator McMahon was later reported as stating that if he had known about the British contribution to the Manhattan Project, the act would have been drafted differently and Britain excluded from its provisions.

In addition to the McMahon Act, further problems arose. Even after that Act, the Combined Policy Committee and Combined Development Trust – two bodies set up under the Quebec Agreement to procure uranium ores and allocate them – continued to function for some time. However, there were serious tensions and the British, who played an important part in worldwide surveys and procurement, had a hard struggle to obtain the annual allocations they needed. They now requested their share to be shipped to them but the Americans resisted this, concerned that there was insufficient ore for their own production. Furthermore, the Americans regarded nuclear technology as being of a cataclysmic or 'end of the world' nature, sole possession of which would render the United States invulnerable to its enemies. At this juncture, some members of the US Senate discovered the existence of the Quebec Agreement. They perceived it as a violation of national sovereignty, which had long been regarded as sacrosanct – particularly among the more conservative elements in US politics – and were vociferous in their opposition to any continuation of nuclear collaboration with Britain.

Despite his dismay at the withdrawal of American collaboration, Prime Minister Clement Attlee was of the firm opinion that without nuclear weapons Britain would be left isolated and powerless in the face of the growing threat of the Soviet Union in Europe, and thus would have to develop her own independently of the United States. He strongly believed that international control of nuclear power should be exercised through the United Nations (UN) but the UN Atomic Energy Commission, which he had been largely instrumental in establishing, failed to reach an agreement over a plan for international control. In the light of this and the McMahon Act, Attlee felt that Britain must acquire the capability to produce nuclear weapons.

The entire programme was contained in the Ministry of Supply, which provided a large and powerful infrastructure together with much experience, gained during the war, in managing research and production establishments and running large scientific projects. Within the ministry, a new Department of Atomic Energy (DATEN) was formed, taking over all the responsibilities of the Directorate of Tube Alloys.

To establish the programme, however, Attlee had to engage the services of four particular men. The first of these was Lord Portal of Hungerford who, as Air Marshal Sir Charles Portal, had been Chief of the Air Staff during the war. A trusted and proven Whitehall operator, he was a practical man as well as being politically minded. He was considered ideal for the task of resolving the problems of obtaining the resources required by the planned nuclear weapon development programme.

In January 1946 Professor John Cockcroft was appointed to head the newly created AERE, which was subsequently located at Harwell, on the border of Berkshire and Oxfordshire; work on the site began in April. Cockcroft was a Nobel Prize winner who had been at the Cavendish Laboratory before the war and had, with Ernest Walton, been the first to split an atom artificially. During the war he had worked in Canada at Chalk River, an Anglo–Canadian–French research establishment that worked on the design and construction of nuclear reactors. After taking up his appointment, Cockcroft proceeded to recruit some of those with whom he had worked at Chalk River.

The British bomb would be based on plutonium and therein lay a problem. During the war, the British scientists working on the Manhattan Project had never been granted admission to the plutonium production plants at Hanford, in Washington State, and were given no information concerning the construction of reactors or plutonium production processes. Nor were they permitted access to the uranium separation plant at Oak Ridge in Tennessee. Unlike uranium, plutonium does not exist in nature – it has to be manufactured, atom by atom, by placing uranium in a nuclear reactor. As the Americans had discovered, the magnitude of the entire Manhattan Project was almost unimaginable. In 1945 it matched the US automobile industry in terms of industrial investment, scale of operations and numbers of people employed. Its cost was estimated at 2 billion dollars, which was equivalent to the cost of sending the first man to the moon.

During the war, Britain had almost exhausted its supplies of ammunition: a crisis that could have had fatal consequences. The situation had been saved by the inspired leadership of one man, an engineer named Christopher Hinton. In January 1946 the government appointed him to take on yet another gargantuan task, that of producing plutonium for the British bomb.

One of the problems facing Hinton was the shortage of qualified engineers. At that time, Britain was facing the massive task of post-war reconstruction and engineers in particular were needed to build up the country's industrial base again, repair the damage caused by six years of war and revive export trade. Furthermore, the number of qualifying engineers had been reduced to almost nil during the war, and so it was extremely difficult to recruit suitably qualified personnel. It was principally for this reason that, during the month following his appointment, Hinton chose to establish his Atomic Energy Production Division in the north of England, at Risley in Lancashire, rather than in the south where he considered he would never find any engineers at all. On starting to look for likely candidates, however, he encountered another problem: as the project was being conducted under the auspices of the Ministry of Supply, all recruitment had to be carried out through the Scientific Civil Service (SCS), whose pay levels were not competitive with those being offered by industry. Furthermore, those scientists and engineers seriously interested in working for the SCS and attracted by nuclear research all tended to want to work at Harwell, which offered more attractive career prospects.

Hinton thus turned to some of the engineers who had worked under him during the war; once again secrecy was paramount and those approached could be told nothing at first. Before long, fourteen individuals gathered at Risley to receive an initial briefing from Dennis Ginns, an engineer who had worked at Chalk River in Canada and who gave his new colleagues a basic introduction to the principles of nuclear energy. As his lecture progressed, those listening to him realized that they were being asked to use chain reactions to release the huge amounts of energy stored in the nucleus according to Einstein's famous equation $E = mc^2$. They also concluded that such a system could provide a possible source of energy for the future; in addition, it was also a possible means of producing the most devastating type of bomb that the world had ever known.

Having undertaken to deliver sufficient plutonium for the first bomb by 1952, Hinton knew that there was no time to be lost and set his team to work, subjecting them to a punishing schedule while he looked for an isolated site for his plutonium factory. Eventually he selected Sellafield in Cumbria on the coast of north-west England. The site was subsequently christened Windscale and, when further land was taken over for additional reactors, the new area was named Calder Hall. Ultimately, the entire area was renamed Sellafield.

Hinton initially wanted to build pressurized graphite-moderated gas-cooled reactors but on advice from Harwell, which advised that design and construction would take too long, decided instead on an air-cooled design in which air passed over the reactor, cooling the uranium fuel rods before being discharged via very tall chimneys. His decision to opt for an air-cooled rather than water-cooled system was based on two facts. Firstly, there was the problem of finding adequate supplies of very pure cooling water. Secondly, there was the risk inherent in using water as a coolant, especially in graphite-moderated reactors. If a reactor overheated and the water turned to steam, the steam would not remove heat so efficiently from the reactor core which would then overheat even more. A further problem, in a 'loss of coolant accident', was that some or all of the moderating effect of the water, slowing down the nuclear reactions, would be lost and a runaway reaction could occur with the risk of a hydrogen explosion (such as that which was to occur at Chernobyl in April 1986). It was for that reason that the Americans had sited their reactors at

Hanford in remote areas. In Hinton's eyes, therefore, graphite water-cooled reactors were unsuitable in a small, highly populated island such as Britain.

This decision brought Hinton into direct conflict with his superiors in the Ministry of Supply, who were convinced that as the Americans were using graphite water-cooled reactors, then Britain should follow the same proven route in order to be able to produce plutonium as soon as possible. Angered at what they saw as intransigence on his part, they were at one point prepared to discipline him but he stood his ground. Adhering to his choice of air-cooled reactors, he opted for a design with tall chimneys 125 metres (410 feet) high through which air would be blown to cool the reactor.

Hinton was advised by scientists at Harwell and by meteorologists that this system would be quite safe because if any air was contaminated while passing through the reactor, by the time it emerged from the chimneys at 410 feet it would be too dispersed to contaminate the atmosphere. Subsequently, however – and by which time building at Windscale was well under way – Harwell had second thoughts, principally as a result of a visit paid by its director, Professor John Cockcroft, to the United States. There, he heard rumours that problems had been experienced with particulate emissions from the chimney of a reactor contaminating the ground in the area. (It later transpired that Cockcroft was mistaken, as the emissions were from a chemical plant at Oak Ridge in Tennessee.) Once made aware of this possible threat, Hinton decided that the chimneys would have to be fitted with filters. However, the chimneys themselves were already half-built and so, with no time available for any delay in the already very tight schedule, the hastily designed huge filter galleries had to be constructed 122 metres (400 feet) up in the air, very near the top of the chimneys. The difficulties of regular maintenance, as well as construction, ultimately proved formidable.

Meanwhile, a further problem had arisen with the high-purity graphite blocks from which the reactors themselves were being constructed. During the machining, Harwell carried out research on the material and discovered that when graphite is heated and irradiated with neutrons, it expands unidirectionally. This would result in distortion of the blocks and narrowing of the channels, preventing insertion of the fuel elements and limiting the life of the reactor to only two years or so. The blocks thus had to be redesigned and in the event worked satisfactorily.

Another problem facing Hinton was that there was no time to assemble a pilot chemical plant; a full-scale one had to be built straightaway. Furthermore, once the manufacturing progress began and the radioactive uranium was beginning to go through the process, it would be impossible for anyone ever to go inside the building to make alterations. The building itself would be vast: 60 metres (200 feet) high and surmounted by a 60-metre (200-foot) chimney.

In March 1946 work began on building a factory at Springfields, near Preston in Lancashire, where uranium ore would be crushed and purified to a very high degree, eliminating any impurities that would otherwise poison the reactor, and turned into uranium metal which was cast into bars. These would be sent either to Windscale in the form of fuel elements for irradiation in the reactors there, or to another facility at Capenhurst, in Cheshire, where the uranium would be fed through a gaseous diffusion plant that gradually separated out the uranium-235 isotope comprising 0.7 per cent of the total in natural uranium, a complex chemical process.

Meanwhile, responsibility for development of the bomb itself had been given to the fourth member of that quartet of remarkable scientists: William Penney. As mentioned earlier, he had been a member of the British contingent working at Los Alamos. One of Britain's team of leading nuclear scientists, he had gained three doctorates by the age of twenty-five. After studying physics at the Imperial College of Science and Technology at the University of London, and at Cambridge University, he had taught at Imperial College from 1936. During the war, he had carried out research for the Ministry of Home Security on the effects of bombing and for the Admiralty on the 'Mulberry' artificial harbours used in the D-Day landings in Normandy in June 1944. On being sent, in December 1943, to the United States, he had been appointed a principal scientific officer at Los Alamos, and was the sole member of the British contingent to witness the bombing of Nagasaki, viewing it from an accompanying aircraft in the company of an RAF officer, Group Captain Leonard Cheshire VC. A few days later, he was sent to visit the city itself to assess the effects of the bomb damage and measure the effects of its blast. He was thus among the first to see the appalling effects of an atomic explosion.

Such was Penney's standing with the Americans that they wanted him to continue working with them on their post-war nuclear development programme. Before conducting the first of a series of test explosions in July 1946 at Bikini Atoll in the Pacific, they asked the British government if they could borrow him because of his expertise in the effects of explosions. Accompanied by a small team of other

British scientists, he played a vital role in these tests, precisely gauging blast and impact effects at different locations.

Penney had intended to return to academic life after the war and had been offered a professorship at Oxford at about the same time as he was approached to develop a British atomic bomb. According to accounts later given by some of his former colleagues, he was concerned about the moral implications of the bomb, although he was convinced of its value as a deterrent. He came under intense pressure from those at senior levels of government who saw him as essential for the success of the project and, after lengthy consideration, gave in and was appointed Chief Superintendent of Armaments Research.

Interestingly, Penney was the only one of the forty British scientists who had worked on the wartime Manhattan Project to be employed on the British bomb itself, although a number took up places at Harwell and elsewhere. There were various reasons for this: some had decided to stay in the United States, while others decided to work at Harwell, which was part of the programme, or return to academic posts held before the war.

In January 1946 Penney took up his post as head of the large armaments research establishment at Fort Halstead, on the Downs south of London. In May 1947 he received his directive concerning the development of an atomic bomb and set about recruiting a team of scientists. During the summer of 1947 he assembled some thirty or so suitably qualified individuals at the Woolwich Arsenal, which was part of his fiefdom. Addressing them in the library, the curtains drawn for security and an armed guard outside the door, by all accounts he opened with the dramatic statement: 'Gentlemen, the Prime Minister has asked me to make an atomic bomb and I want you to help me.' The information that Penney proceeded to divulge was a complete revelation to those gathered together that day. Although it was two years since the end of the war, only a certain amount of information had been released about the bombs dropped on Hiroshima and Nagasaki. This had maintained that both were relatively crude devices based on what was called the 'gun method': this in essence comprised a gun-type barrel assembly containing two sub-critical pieces of uranium-235. One was fired into the other, the latter being precision-machined to accept it. At the moment of impact, the entire mass of uranium became supercritical and initiated a chain reaction.

What had not been revealed was that the bomb dropped on Nagasaki had been of a different type, an implosion-initiated device in which a spherical core of plutonium was squeezed by high explosive into one supercritical mass, initiating the chain reaction. The squeezing effect had to be instantaneous and uniform over the whole surface of the sphere and this was achieved, as Penney was able to tell those listening to him that day, by a system developed at Los Alamos during the war: the use of multi-point detonation and explosive lenses. Simultaneous firing of a number of detonators produced inward pressure, squeezing the sphere uniformly. Meanwhile, similar in principle to a spectacle lens that corrects the passage of light so that it strikes the eye in the correct spot, each explosive lens corrected the inward travelling pressure wave until it formed the correct shape that produced the perfect squeeze.

Among those approached by Penney was John Challens, an electronics specialist who in 1936 had joined the research department at the Master General of the

Ordnance's department at Woolwich; he had spent the war working on guns and rockets, much of it at a rocket range at Abercore in western Wales. Challens accepted and was subsequently responsible for the task of developing the electronic firing system for the new bomb.

Another recruit, who worked under Challens, was Eddie Howse who during the war had worked on radar at Malvern and Rugby. In 1948 he was posted to Fort Halstead, where his first task was to design a pulse transformer without knowing the reason for doing so. He laughed when remembering those early days: 'The secrecy never worried me because I went straight from college to working on radar and took the Official Secrets Act at that stage and after that, everything I did was secret. When I first met my wife-to-be, the only question I asked her was whether her father was a member of the Communist Party. She said no and I said, "Well, that's all right, I can marry you then."'

Other recruits to Penney's team included mathematical physicist John Corner; Roy Pilgrim, an expert in blast measurement who had worked with Penney at the American Bikini Atoll test; metallurgist Graham Hopkin; electronics and instrumentation experts L. C. Tyte, Charles Adams and Ieuan Maddock; explosives experts Ernie Mott and Bill Moyce; health and safety specialists David Barnes and Geoffrey Dale; chemist Dai Lewis; as well as radiochemist Frank Morgan. Recruiting for the team was difficult and took a great deal of time. As John Challens recalled: 'I spent a lot of time on interviewing boards. The real problem was you couldn't tell the candidate what you wanted him for. And a lot of people weren't prepared to take you on trust.'

All candidates underwent a lengthy series of interviews during which they were told nothing about the work involved or the appointments for which they were being considered. Eventually, however, a team was assembled and started work. This was subsequently augmented by a team of Royal Air Force (RAF) officers headed by Wing Commander John Rowlands. Its role was to ensure that the bomb was designed in such a way that the RAF could store, service, transport and, if necessary, use it. Furthermore, the team would ultimately have to advise the Air Ministry on the construction of buildings for secure storage and servicing of such weapons, as well as specialist equipment and training of RAF personnel in handling of them. All science graduates, members of the team were attached to each of the departments established by Penney.

Secrecy was paramount and Penney and his scientists worked in a virtual state of quarantine, as Clement Attlee had made it clear that he did not want anyone knowing that Britain was developing its own atomic weapon. This placed severe limitations on the scientists when, for example, they were talking to colleagues at Woolwich Arsenal who were not involved in projects connected with the nuclear bomb programme. At the same time, efforts to obtain resources were hampered by the fact that key people could not be approached as they were not permitted to know the reason for such requirements. This inevitably prevented the programme from enjoying the priority it had been accorded. An example of this was that Lord Portal was issued by Attlee with a series of letters of authority which would have greatly facilitated the obtaining of resources, but could not use them as he was unable to divulge the existence of the programme.

Short of personnel, resources and technical information, the entire programme was racing against the clock to keep to the deadline set by the government. In order to try and alleviate the problems under which it was labouring, Clement Attlee decided to approach the Americans in a final attempt to enlist their help.

Unlike the United States, which had greatly profited from the Second World War, Britain was virtually bankrupt. Despite their so-called 'special relationship', the British had been forced to buy or lease every ship, aircraft, tank and weapon obtained from the United States, which itself did not enter the war until 1941. By this time Britain had been standing virtually alone in opposing the might of the Axis powers. The country was on its knees after six years of suffering and privations. Attlee later summed up the reasons for Britain's parlous state and how to rectify it: 'We alone, of all the nations, went through two great wars. We stood alone. For that fight we put everything in that we had. We sacrificed all our wealth overseas. We converted all our industries and that is why we are left in this position today. The only way out is by greater output of all the things that we need. And that means harder work.'

At the end of the war, in order to finance its desperately needed programme of reconstruction, Britain had negotiated a 7.5-billion-dollar loan from the United States. By 1947, however, the remaining amount available was 500 million dollars and so the country was close to bankruptcy. At that time the US Secretary of State, George Marshall, had proposed the Marshall Plan, which would fund the rebuilding of Europe and Britain. As mentioned earlier the Americans were, however, determined to exercise a monopoly on nuclear technology in general. Now they decided to force Britain to surrender its share of the uranium ore and forget about the Quebec and Hyde Park Agreements.

Refusal to do so would result in withholding of further financial aid. This demand was made in negotiations in December 1947, during which it was also made clear to the British that there would be no further sharing of technological information (although this was in any case forbidden by the McMahon Act) unless they complied.

Horrified and angered not only by the United States' refusal to continue sharing nuclear technology but also by the outrageous use of such blackmail, the British had no choice but to agree to the Americans' demands. These negotiations did, however, lead to a *modus vivendi* a month later which continued the arrangements for joint procurement of uranium supplies and for co-operation in nine areas of nuclear research. Despite this, however, Clement Attlee was even more determined that Britain must have its own atomic bomb.

One of Attlee's other major concerns was that the press would discover the existence of the programme and publicize it. Such was the degree of security that the government was unable to issue a D-Notice, the mechanism by which the voluntary co-operation of the press is obtained over matters of national security. In May 1948 it was decided instead to issue a guarded statement about Britain producing an atomic bomb, in return for which it would expect the press to comply with a D-Notice that would block any further discussion of the subject. In the House of Commons, in reply to a question concerning development weapons put forward by a primed backbench member of parliament, a minister issued a statement declaring that research and development was of a high priority and that development of all types of weapons, including atomic ones, was taking place. At the precise moment that the statement was being made, editors throughout Fleet Street were being issued with copies of a D-Notice stating that they could not engage in any investigation, reporting or discussion of any sort relating to the development of British atomic weapons.

As explained earlier, in an atomic bomb there are two ways of achieving an atomic explosion: the gun and implosion methods. In a Hiroshima-type bomb, two sub-critical pieces of uranium-235 in a gun-like assembly were shot together so that they suddenly formed a supercritical mass and exploded. This would not work in a bomb using plutonium-239, which is more reactive and liable to predetonate, resulting in an ineffective partial explosion. Thus the implosion method was used for the Nagasaki-type plutonium bomb; a sphere of plutonium was enclosed in a much larger sphere made up of carefully shaped charges of conventional high explosive which, when detonated, compressed the plutonium-239 so that it became supercritical and an atomic explosion occurred. The implosion method was more efficient but extremely difficult to design.

In the United States during the war, one of the British scientists who helped to solve many of the problems in achieving success with implosion techniques was Dr Klaus Fuchs. As mentioned earlier, he was a German émigré, who had studied physics and mathematics at the universities of Leipzig and Kiel. Forced to flee when the Nazis came to power in 1933, he made his way to Britain where he studied at the University of Edinburgh from which he received his doctorate. In 1940, however, along with thousands of others classed as 'aliens', he was interned and subsequently transported to Canada. By the end of the year, however, he had been released and returned to Britain. In the spring of

1941 he was invited by Professor Rudolf Peierls to join him at Birmingham University. Naturalized British in 1942, Fuchs was employed in the Tube Alloys programme until late 1943, when he was recruited for the Manhattan Project and sent to the United States where he contributed a great deal to the theory and design of the plutonium bomb. On returning to Britain in the summer of 1946, he became head of the theoretical physics department at Harwell.

At this time, it was suspected that the Soviet Union was in the process of developing an atomic bomb and Britain's Secret Intelligence Service (SIS) was devoting considerable resources to gleaning sufficient intelligence to be able to esti-mate a production timescale. Despite the somewhat shabby treatment accorded to Britain by the United States over nuclear matters, the two countries were still co-operating over matters of intelligence. In 1948, the SIS supplied the Americans with reports based on deciphered Soviet inter-cepts relating to atomic weapon experiments. The United States meanwhile mounted an operation, codenamed Project Snifden, using specially equipped US Air Force WB-29 aircraft to conduct airborne monitoring around the periph-ery of Russian airspace in the Soviet Far East while ostensibly carrying out meteorological survey flights.

On 29 August 1949 the first Soviet atom bomb test took place and it was not long before a WB-29, on a flight in the area of Kamchatka, detected a cloud of radioactivity. A few days later, an RAF Halifax aircraft collected samples of radioactive fall-out over the Atlantic.

The evidence was irrefutable but many in America, including some scientists and General Leslie Groves, generally held the Soviet Union in contempt and were cer-tain that the Soviets would not be able to develop a bomb for many years. The only exception was one non-nuclear scientist, a Nobel laureate named Irving Langmuir, who had a high regard for Soviet scientists and had predicted that the Soviets would be in possession of a bomb within five years of the end of the war. President Harry S. Truman, who was not a technically educated man, refused to believe that the Russians could have tested a bomb and persisted in holding discussions with his staff during which he put forward the theory that the explosion could have been caused by a reactor blowing up because of faulty design.

Even when presented with definite intelligence confirming that it was a bomb and that it had been of a similar design to the implosion type (nicknamed 'Fat Man') dropped on Nagasaki, he insisted that the Atomic Energy Commission officials presenting the information to him sign the document, confirming that they believed the information to be true. On 23 September 1949, Truman announced to the world that the Soviet Union had exploded an atomic bomb.

In view of previous predictions by both the SIS and the newly formed Central Intelligence Agency (CIA) that the Soviets would not possess an atomic weapon before 1953, the revelation of the test was not only a shock to both organizations but also a possible indication of treachery on the part of persons unknown. In the United States the Federal Bureau of Investigation (FBI) swiftly mounted a major operation to determine whether Russia's unexpected triumph was in any way connected to Alan Nunn May, a British scientist who had worked on the Tube Alloys programme in Britain before being transferred to Chalk River in Canada.

In September 1945 a defector from the Soviet embassy in Ottawa, a cipher clerk named Igor Gouzenko, had revealed that Nunn May had passed information to the Soviet Union while working at Chalk River. Nunn May had been recruited by Colonel Nikolai Zabotin, an officer in the Soviet military intelligence service, the Main Intelligence Directorate of the General Staff, better known by its acronym GRU. Zabotin, who operated under the diplomatic cover of military attaché, had contacted him not long after his arrival at Chalk River and thereafter contact had been maintained through another GRU officer, Pavel Angelov. During the following two and a half years, Nunn May paid a number of visits to other establishments involved in atomic research, including the Argonne Laboratory in Chicago. Indeed, security officials there became suspicious of the frequency of his visits and eventually refused his further requests for access.

By the beginning of 1946 Nunn May had returned to Britain, where he took up a post at London University. By then he was attempting to sever contact with the Soviets but in March he was arrested and confessed everything. On 1 May 1946 he was sentenced to ten years' imprisonment. It later transpired that he had been an avowed Communist while at Cambridge University but, inexplicably, had not been vetted before being recruited for the Tube Alloys project.

While the FBI sought to confirm whether there had been any traitors among those who had worked on the Manhattan Project, American cryptographers of the US Armed Forces Security Agency (AFSA), later the National Security Agency (NSA), were decrypting wartime Soviet cable transmissions between the United States and Moscow. This was part of a major codebreaking operation called 'Venona' which began in 1946 and by mid-1947 revealed evidence of a massive Soviet espionage operation in the

United States during the war. Shortly after President Truman's announcement, the AFSA decrypted two intercepts: one of these was a summary of a Manhattan Project document while the other identified the author and source as the British scientist Dr Klaus Fuchs.

Investigation of Fuchs's background by the Security Service, popularly known as MI5, revealed that he was a member of a family well known in Germany as active Communists. Having joined the German Communist Party in 1930, he had fled Nazi Germany for Britain three years later on the party's orders, his left-wing sympathies being recorded on his arrival and passed to the Security Service. Further evidence of his membership of the Communist Party came a year later when the Security Service received a letter from the Chief Constable of the police in Bristol; he had been informed by the German consul in the city that Fuchs was living with a family of suspected Communists and that he was a Soviet agent. Bearing in mind the biased source of this report, this information had been ignored.

A second report on Fuchs had been received from a Security Service informer within the German refugee community who had revealed Fuchs's Communist connections and his activities in Germany before 1933. The Security Service, heavily involved in investigating subversive organizations at the time, had not checked further on Fuchs, but the officer in charge of its Communist Section had written a report stating that he was more likely to betray secrets to the Russians than to the Germans and had advised that he should not be allowed any more access to secrets than was strictly necessary.

Fuchs was thus accorded a low security rating but unfortunately the Security Service was unaware of the exact nature of his work at the time and did not communicate its recommendations to his employers. Moreover, for unexplained reasons, it did not do so when he was transferred to the United States in 1943 to work on the Manhattan Project; when completing an American security questionnaire about him, it merely stated that he was 'politically inactive and unobjectionable'.

Fuchs returned to Britain and his work at Harwell. Before this, the Security Service had carried out a five-month-long investigation into him but found nothing. Had it checked with the Canadian security authorities, it would have discovered that one of his associates while interned in Canada was a well-known German Communist named Hans Kahle, who was a suspected Russian agent and who in 1945 was spotted in East Germany working for the Soviets.

Following the decryption of the Venona intercept, Fuchs's telephone was tapped and his mail intercepted. He was questioned but revealed nothing until 24 January 1950, when one of his interrogators suggested that he might be permitted to remain at Harwell if he admitted to any wrongdoing. This ploy worked and he confessed, revealing that he had started supplying information to the Soviets from late 1941, while working on the Tube Alloys project under Rudolf Peierls at Birmingham University. He had contacted the leader of the underground German Communist Party in Britain, Jürgen Kuczynski, for assistance in passing on information to the Soviets, and Kuczynski had put him in contact with Simon Kremer, a GRU officer based at the Soviet residency in London. Fuchs was subsequently handed on to another GRU officer named Ursula Beurton, the sister of Jürgen Kuczynski. Operating under the codename of 'Sonya', and living in the Oxfordshire town of Chipping

Norton, her cover was that of a Jewish refugee from Germany named Mrs Brewer. Beurton was to remain undetected in Britain until 1947, when she was questioned by the Security Service after being named by a Soviet intelligence officer, Alexander Foote, who had defected to Britain earlier that year. She succeeded, however, in convincing her interrogator, William 'Jim' Skardon, of her innocence and thus was not placed under surveillance. Two days later she disappeared and surfaced some years later in East Germany, having been made an honorary colonel in the Red Army in recognition of her achievements on behalf of the GRU.

After Fuchs's arrival in the United States in late 1943, control of him as an agent had been transferred from the GRU to the Soviet security police (KGB). His controller was Anatoly Yakovlev, a KGB officer acting under the diplomatic cover of a Soviet vice-consul in New York, with whom he communicated via a Swiss-born courier named Harry Gold whom he first met on 5 February 1944. Based in New York until the latter part of 1944, Fuchs passed a considerable amount of information to the Soviets before being posted to Los Alamos in New Mexico. It was not until February 1945, when he had returned to New York on holiday, that he had been able to re-establish contact with Gold.

Following his return to Britain in 1946 and taking up his new post at Harwell, Fuchs had continued to work for the Soviets, passing information to his KGB controller in London. It appears, however, that by the time of the period leading up to his arrest his enthusiasm for such work had waned, possibly due to the fact that he had by then developed an increasing respect and affection for his adopted country.

Immediately after confessing, Fuchs was arrested and on 2 February 1950 charged with espionage. His trial took place on 10 February, lasting exactly one and a half hours; he was convicted and sentenced on the same day to fourteen years' imprisonment. At the time, the political ramifications of his treachery were far-reaching and caused huge embarrassment to Britain. It appeared that a major lapse in British security had not only compromised the Americans but also enabled the Soviet Union to develop its own atomic bomb and thus achieve apparent parity within a very short time.

In fact, Fuchs was not the only Soviet agent working inside the Anglo–American nuclear weapon programmes. At least three other members of the Tube Alloys project in Britain, one identified only by the letter 'K' and the other two by their Soviet codenames of 'Moor' and 'Kelly', had reportedly passed information to the Soviets. Meanwhile, as already mentioned, the Soviets also succeeded in penetrating the Anglo–Canadian nuclear research project at Chalk River in Canada through their recruitment of Alan Nunn May and others. In the United States an American scientist working on the Manhattan Project, identified only by the codename 'Mar', was recruited by the Soviets in April 1943 and by December of that year had passed on details of the construction of reactors, cooling systems, production of plutonium and protection against radiation. Others were also recruited: one was a scientist in the radiation laboratory at Berkeley, in California, while another worked in the Manhattan Project's metallurgical laboratory at Chicago University. A third was a construction engineer who passed on information about plant and equipment used in the project.

In addition to Fuchs, the Soviets had two other agents within Los Alamos, both recruited in November 1944. The first was a machinist, an Army sergeant named David

Greenglass who was recruited via his wife, the sister of a woman named Ethel Rosenberg. The latter, along with her husband Julius, an engineer in the US Army's Signal Corps, headed a ring of Soviet spies in the United States before both were arrested in May 1950, together with Greenglass and another conspirator named Morton Sobell, shortly after Harry Gold had been apprehended. Brought to trial in March 1951, both were subsequently convicted of espionage and sentenced to death. They were executed at Sing Sing Prison on 19 June 1953. Greenglass, who appeared as the chief prosecution witness, was sentenced to fifteen years' imprisonment while Harry Gold and Morton Sobell were each sentenced to thirty years'.

The second Soviet agent in Los Alamos was a brilliant nineteen-year-old physicist named Theodore 'Ted' Hall who, it is believed, was the first to reveal the secrets of the implosion method to the Soviets. Both he and Fuchs are thought to have independently provided Moscow with the plans of the American bomb and to have given the date of the first test at Alamogordo which was scheduled for 10 July 1945 (although in the event it was delayed for six days by bad weather). Hall subsequently supplied the Soviets with the results of the test and such was the mass of detail in the information supplied by him, Fuchs and the other Soviet spies within the Manhattan Project that the first atomic weapon exploded by the Soviet Union was an exact replica of the 'Fat Man' bomb produced at Los Alamos.

Meanwhile, Christopher Hinton and his team at Windscale were experiencing further problems with the reactors, caused by faulty information supplied by Harwell on graphite, neutron flux and filtration. The core of each reactor comprised a precision-machined block of extremely pure graphite pierced with holes in which rods of uranium were placed. When enough rods were placed close together, a spontaneous nuclear combustion began. The fission chain reaction would in time consume some of the uranium-235 atoms contained in the fuel and convert some of the uranium-238 atoms to plutonium. The graphite block, while providing the structure containing the uranium rods, also acted as a moderator, slowing down the neutrons and thus increasing the probability of their hitting an atomic nucleus. However, successful operation all depended on a sufficient quantity of neutrons being released in the fission process.

Tom Tuohy was manager in charge of the reactors, or 'piles' as they were called, and it was his task to carry out all the necessary measurements leading to criticality, as he later recalled: 'When uranium was loaded and a measurement was necessary, it didn't matter what time of the day or night – I was in there with my second-in-command, taking the necessary measurements to go up to criticality. If the reactor was going to produce enough plutonium for a bomb, the chain reaction would have to start when a very specific amount of uranium fuel had been loaded.' The amount that had been forecast was approximately 42 tons; in the event, it proved to be 102 tons.

Until then, Penney had assumed that Windscale would not only produce the plutonium but also carry out the difficult process of forming it into the sphere which would form the core of the bomb. With the plant experiencing such problems, however, he realized that he would have to set up another facility to manufacture the core. This was built at the new weapons site at Aldermaston, in Berkshire, to which High Explosive Research (the early code name for the atomic weapon development programme) had begun to move from Fort Halstead in April 1950. Penney and his team were well aware of the hazards of plutonium and developed safe methods for handling it. Reputedly the most dangerous of metals, it is silvery grey in colour and oxidizes quickly on exposure to air, producing a very fine-particled oxide. If this is inhaled and lodges in the lungs, is ingested and lodges in other parts of the body or gets into the bloodstream through an open wound, it can cause serious problems leading to cancers.

A specially designed building housed the area in which the material would be handled, with special ventilation systems and corridors designed to ensure that no leakage could occur from it. Personnel working in it wore pressurized suits with integral breathing systems; initially manufactured from heavy black neoprene rubber, these were known as 'frog suits' as they resembled the diving suits worn by frogmen and indeed were developed from such.

By now it was 1951, and the general election of that year saw the Conservative Party returned to power with Winston Churchill once again taking up office as Prime Minister. Hitherto he had been unaware of the existence of the post-war nuclear weapon development programme which had so far cost 100 million pounds; such was his enthusiasm when he learned of it that he endorsed October 1952 as the date for the testing of Britain's first atomic bomb. During the following months, diplomatic efforts were put in hand to pave the way for the tests to take place in the area of the Montebello Islands off the north-west coast of Australia.

By the early summer of 1951, construction of the two reactors at Windscale had been completed and the loading of the fuel elements took place. Just as the reactors were about to be started up, however, devastating news arrived from Harwell. The theoreticians had suddenly realized their original calculations were incorrect and that the piles would in practice operate much less efficiently than planned. The reactors would simply not make plutonium quickly enough to meet the deadlines. A major redesign would involve years of delay and was out of the question. A radical solution was needed.

The Harwell calculations had missed one crucial factor: many of the neutrons that should have been colliding with uranium nuclei and converting them to plutonium would instead simply be absorbed by the aluminium casings surrounding the uranium fuel rods. The casings each had fourteen cooling fins. The engineers calculated that if these fins could be trimmed very slightly, the reduction in aluminium would bring the reactor back to up to full power. But the reactor contained 36,000 uranium fuel assemblies, a total of 504,000 fins. Undaunted by the magnitude of the task, the engineers built special rigs and worked round the clock to clip 1.6 millimetres (a sixteenth of an inch) off every single fin. At the same time, small graphite 'boats' were produced at Windscale's workshops to narrow the fuel channels in the reactor and increase the reactivity in the pile. Within three weeks, the entire process had been completed and the fuel reloaded into the reactors. The measure worked: the first reactor went critical in October 1951 and the second in June the following year.

The process of producing plutonium starts when sufficient uranium is inserted into a reactor to start a fission reaction. A chain reaction begins when a uranium atom splits and ejects a number of neutrons which then either split other atoms or are absorbed by them. The process is regulated by the use of control rods, made of neutron-absorbing material, which can be motored into the pile core gradually or slowly withdrawn. By controlling the process the number of fissions can be maintained at a steady level. The fuel elements have to be left in the reactor for a sufficient length of time to produce the desired plutonium-239 but not for too long or the result will be plutonium-240 which is not an efficient explosive.

With the problem of production solved, Christopher Hinton and his team started to manufacture plutonium. Although there were still fifteen months to the test date, much remained to be done. Firstly, the reactor had to be run long enough for plutonium to be produced in the fuel elements, which then had to be extracted from the reactor, dissolved and put through the separation plant to separate out the small amounts of plutonium from the large quantities of leftover uranium and other by-products. Thereafter, the plutonium would have to be purified, turned into metal and machined into hemispheres to form the bomb's core.

By August 1952, despite the continual setbacks that had plagued it, Windscale had produced sufficient plutonium to meet the deadline set for the test, which was codenamed 'Hurricane'. Slugs of plutonium, each in its own sealed cylindrical container, were packed into a drum which was sealed and loaded aboard an Army truck on which it was despatched to Aldermaston. On its arrival, the drum was checked for gamma radiation before being unloaded and wheeled on a trolley into Building A1, where it was taken into one of the newly constructed laboratories.

Building A1 was designed for the manufacture of plutonium cores and consisted of three elements. The operating corridor comprised a glove box, a stainless-steel structure equipped with a 12-millimetre-thick ($1/2$-inch) Perspex window, allowing engineers and other operatives to see what they were doing, and sealed apertures equipped with arm-length rubber latex gloves to enable them to carry out their work from the outside while fully protected. Fully airtight, it was filled with inert argon gas to prevent oxidation of the plutonium. Behind it was a large stainless-steel room, measuring some 6 metres (20 feet) wide by some 18.5 metres (60 feet) long, from which the rear of the glove box could be accessed by the engineers and from where modifications to equipment could be carried out or new equipment installed. This room was subject to contamination and thus only personnel wearing 'frog suits' could enter it. Above these two areas was a floor containing the banks of high-efficiency filters. As the filters would need changing periodically, this floor was also considered to be a contaminated area where 'frog suits' needed to be worn. In addition to these three areas, there were adjacent laboratories providing support for the main laboratory. Nearby was the complex's other building which housed administrative offices and other laboratory facilities.

Up until now, the scientists at Aldermaston had only been working on experiments with small pieces of plutonium. With the arrival of the material from Windscale, they were able to start producing the hemispheres that would comprise the core of the bomb. The pieces of plutonium were placed inside the glove box and weighed before being passed to the next stage where they were cut up and placed in a crucible for melting prior to casting. At this point a blue halo-like flame developed over one of the quantities of molten plutonium, and it was feared that a critical reaction was developing which would have resulted in death or injury to those working in the immediate vicinity. Fortunately, however, the flame (which was later thought to have perhaps been caused by some impurity in the argon gas in the glove box) died away shortly afterwards and the process continued with the plutonium being poured into casts. Once they had cooled, the plutonium hemispheres were broken out of their moulds and on the following day placed in dies and pressed into shape, a process that removed any fissures and cavities on the surface of the metal. Any excess material was then trimmed off with a small lathe before each hemisphere was clad in gold foil, which was then cold-welded. All these processes took place at different stations within the glove box.

A problem occurred, however, when two frog-suited engineers attempted to bring out the completed hemispheres from the contaminated stainless-steel room. Entrance and exit was via a venturi (a short tube inserted into a wider pipeline), which was used to maintain airflows, and then through two heavy steel doors that sealed off the chamber. On this occasion, however, both doors jammed and the two men, together with the two hemispheres in containers, were trapped inside. One door was eventually opened but the other refused to move. Eventually, some two hours later, the water seal pit at the bottom of the door was drained, allowing a gap of about 45 centimetres (18 inches). Through this the plutonium hemispheres could be passed out in their containers, and the two engineers could escape. Afterwards, an escape hatch was installed to cater for any similar mishap in the future.

By now time was running short and the decision was taken to despatch two plutonium cores, comprising four hemispheres, by air to the test site in the Montebello Islands, off the coast of north-west Australia, a journey of some 16,000 kilometres (10,000 miles). The task of escorting them was given to Wing Commander John Rowlands, the head of the RAF team. Packed in four sealed steel containers, one hemisphere in each, the plutonium cores and a neutron initiator were driven in two unmarked furniture vans from Aldermaston to the RAF base at Lyneham in Wiltshire, accompanied by Rowlands, another RAF officer and a scientist, Bill Moyce, travelling in a staff car. On arrival, the entire consignment was loaded aboard a Hastings transport aircraft and, together with the three men, set off on its journey. A number of contingencies had been taken into consideration, including the possibility of the aircraft crashing; in that event Rowlands, his accompanying officer, Moyce, and the aircrew would have been required to bale out with the four containers, which had been designed to float. Meanwhile, to distract any unwelcome publicity, a decoy aircraft carrying William Penney and a set of dummy containers had taken off at the same time as Rowlands's aircraft and flew to Australia.

As it happened, the journey proved uneventful as the aircraft flew via Cyprus, Sharjah in the Persian Gulf and Ceylon (now Sri Lanka) to Singapore. There the consignment, the two officers and Moyce were transferred to a Sunderland flying boat and flown to the Montebello Islands. On 18 September the aircraft landed on the Montebello lagoon, taxiing to a position alongside HMS *Plym*, the River Class frigate which contained the bomb and inside which it would be exploded.

Three months beforehand, while Aldermaston had been producing the bomb's core, a Royal Navy task force had assembled at the naval base at Chatham, in Kent. This comprised an aircraft carrier, HMS *Campania*, which would act as flagship; two landing ships, HMS *Zeebrugge* and HMS *Narvik*, carrying a detachment of Royal Engineers and their heavy plant and equipment; a third landing ship, HMS *Tracker*, which would be the health control ship; and the River Class frigate HMS *Plym*, complete with a specially designed and extensively equipped weapon room in which the unarmed bomb would be transported and ultimately exploded. All the vessels were specially converted and fitted out in complete secrecy at shipyards at Birkenhead and Chatham and on the Clyde.

The flotilla would have to provide complete support for all personnel involved in the tests. They would be based for three months on the islands, which were uninhabited and had no resources whatsoever, not even fresh water. In addition to food and accommodation, transport would have to be provided to ferry scientists to different locations on the islands, where a vast range of equipment would be sited to record the effects of the explosion.

Meanwhile, much preparatory work had been taking place on the islands with generous help from Australia. The Australian Army provided support with civil engineering and construction tasks, assisted by Royal Engineers who sailed from Britain in February 1952. From October 1951 onwards, the Royal Australian Navy (RAN) and the Australian Weather Bureau had begun meteorological observations. The RAN also surveyed and charted the islands and their surrounding waters, and sited buoys and moorings. In addition it would assist in ferrying passengers and supplies, provide a weather vessel and patrol the area before and after the test. Moreover, three Australian scientists would take part in the test, one of them being Professor E. W. Titterton, Professor of Physics at the Australian National University, who would participate as an expert in telemetry. Ultimately, it was agreed that Professor L. H. Martin, the Defence Scientific Adviser, and W. A. S. Butement, Chief Scientist at the Australian Department of Supply, would join him as senior observers.

During the weeks prior to the flotilla's departure, all the equipment required for the test, including the bomb itself minus its plutonium core and neutron initiator, was loaded aboard the vessels along with a large contingent of scientists, physicists, engineers, mathematicians, doctors, chemists and botanists, each of whom had a positive role to play in the test. In June 1952, led by HMS *Campania*, the task force set sail for the Montebello Islands.

The voyage took eight weeks, during which much work was carried out checking, testing, repacking and stowing equipment ready for use after arrival. Conditions on board the ships were overcrowded and uncomfortable and some of the scientists suffered badly from seasickness. On 8 August HMS *Campania* and the rest of the flotilla arrived and anchored in an area east of the Montebello lagoon; thereafter preparations for the test proceeded apace. On the same day, the Australian government declared the Montebello Islands and a surrounding area of 64 kilometres (40 miles) radius a prohibited area for safety and security reasons.

It was predicted that the proposed underwater detonation, if it achieved an explosive power similar to that of the Nagasaki bomb, would result in a fireball rising high into the atmosphere and taking with it a vast column of water and sand, weighing 10,000 to 100,000 tons, as well as fission products, bomb constituents and many tons of steel from the ship, some of which would be vaporized. Due to the huge weight of water drawn up into the column, fall-out would be produced quickly and within a few thousand yards from the site of the explosion. Most of the radioactivity would be dispersed in the sea around the islands, and would be of high levels only in the area of the explosion and for a short duration afterwards.

Meteorological conditions, particularly wind direction and strength, would be crucial to the safety aspects of the test, particularly with regard to the Australian mainland which lay 75 kilometres (47 miles) to the south-east of the islands. Wind conditions on the west coast of Australia had been studied for two years, and it had been discovered that of ten days in October when other conditions, such as tides, were suitable, there would probably be no more than three when the wind would be blowing away from the mainland. Meteorological forecasts would be provided by the RAN weather vessel and by Royal Australian Air Force (RAAF) bases at Pearce Onslow and Port Hedland.

The safety criteria for protecting the mainland, the flotilla and the site of the main island base specified acceptable wind directions and speeds at surface level and altitudes of 1,525 metres (5,000 feet) and 9,145 metres (30,000 feet). They also dictated that no air up to 1,525 metres (5,000 feet) must reach the mainland within a period of ten hours after the explosion, this allowing for heavy particles of fall-out borne by winds of low strengths to fall into the sea. Following the test, airborne monitoring of atmospheric radioactivity would be carried out at high and low altitudes by RAAF aircraft fitted with detection equipment.

All was in place for initial test rehearsals on 12 and 13 September, a full rehearsal taking place six days later on 18 September, the day of the arrival of Wing Commander John Rowlands's party and the two plutonium cores. On 22 September, William Penney also arrived and final preparations for the test intensified.

Penney and his scientists had designed the bomb so that the initiator and core could be kept separate from it until the last possible moment. It had been decided to position the bomb on a ship, below the waterline, as part of an additional test to determine the effect of a nuclear bomb, planted by a hostile force, exploding aboard a vessel in a major port such as Liverpool or the London. On 2 October, the day before the test, the ship's complement were disembarked, less a small skeleton crew comprising an officer and a small group of sailors who would take the target vessel to the test location. Also remaining on board were Wing Commander John Rowlands and a team of scientists, led by John Challens, who were responsible for carrying out the final procedures for arming the bomb. They were accompanied by Eddie Howse, whose overall responsibility within the project had been the design of the firing circuits but who on this occasion was responsible for liaising between the firing control team on one of the Montebello Islands and those aboard the warship.

By the day before the test, HMS *Plym* was stationed at her predetermined location. It was Wing Commander Rowlands's responsibility to assemble the plutonium core, which he did by using a portable vacuum glove box to extract the two hemispheres and the marble-sized polonium-beryllium neutron initiator, known as an 'urchin', from their respective containers. He had previously conducted a number of criticality experiments at Aldermaston, using a special machine which, surrounded by monitoring equipment, had brought two hemispheres together approximately 2.5 micrometres (a thousandth of an inch) at a time until they were touching. In the event of criticality beginning, a release mechanism would have dropped one hemisphere immediately away from the other.

Having inserted the initiator into a recess in one of the hemispheres, Rowlands carefully assembled the entire plutonium sphere and screwed it into the 'gauntlet', a device for holding the sphere so that it was located precisely in the centre of the bomb. The final component was a high-explosive cartridge which was screwed on to the gauntlet before the entire assembly was slowly lowered, using a small hoist, into the bomb and secured in position. By this time it was just after midnight in the early hours of 3 October; firing of the bomb was only a few hours away.

Wing Commander John Rowlands then disembarked and was transferred to HMS *Campania* as the team of scientists under John Challens continued with arming the bomb. This was not a particularly easy task as the HMS *Plym*'s hold was very limited in size, while the bomb measured 1.5 metres (5 feet) in diameter. They first had to insert all the thirty-two detonator units, each the size of a small coconut and containing two 'exploding wire' detonators. The weapon's initiation system, comprising two firing circuits, had a large degree of redundancy built into it so that if there was a detonator failure on one circuit, the detonator on the other circuit would take its place. Once the thirty-two detonator units were all in place, a total of sixty-four firing cables had to be connected up. Once that lengthy and tedious process was complete, all but John Challens, Eddie

Howse and three members of the ship's crew disembarked from the vessel.

The final task was to connect the two firing circuits to the bomb's power units, which were in turn connected to banks of batteries. As Challens connected the power units to the batteries, Howse was in communication with the control centre, which was monitoring power voltage readings transmitted from the ship to the control centre by telemetry. Acting as a link, he advised Challens on each reading until all were correct. Once all connections had been made, three switches were pressed and Challen inserted a master plug which completed all the circuits in the bomb ready for firing. At approximately 4 a.m., Challens, Howse and the three remaining crew then disembarked from HMS *Plym* in pitch darkness to a launch that took them to one of the islands 10 kilometres (6 miles) away, where an underground control room and bunkers had been constructed by British Army sappers.

Challens carried with him a second master safety plug which, on his arrival ashore, he delivered to the control room. This was inserted into the firing system and all was ready for the test to take place. Meanwhile, all personnel changed into special clothing and took their places in the control room and bunkers. At 9.15 a.m. local time, the firing switch was pressed and three seconds later a massive column of water rose swiftly and silently into the sky, the top of it forming into a huge cloud. Almost half a minute passed before the noise of the explosion, which had the force of 20 kilotons, reached the ears of those who emerged from the bunkers, watching the cloud as a tremor shook the ground around them. Shortly afterwards, it was announced that the test had been a total success.

Despite all the difficulties, Britain had succeeded in developing and exploding its own atomic bomb. Three weeks later, however, the United States exploded the first thermonuclear weapon, a hydrogen bomb device that was a thousand times more powerful than the British weapon. The Americans' decision to proceed with its development without delay stemmed from their belief that Klaus Fuchs had also provided the Soviets with information concerning thermonuclear technology. By 1957 Britain, fully committed to being a nuclear power, had also tested its own hydrogen bomb. This was undoubtedly the principal factor that led to the United States deciding that the wartime 'special relationship' was worth reviving after all.

DISMANTLING THE BOMB

or almost fifty years the world lived in the shadow of the threat of nuclear conflict. With the end of the Cold War, it appeared that the threat of mutual destruction might have been avoided. In the wake of arms reduction, however, a major problem arose: how to dispose of many thousands of nuclear weapons.

The nuclear arms race had its early beginnings during the Second World War when, as described in 'A Very British Bomb', first the United States and then the Soviet Union began their respective atomic weapons development programmes. On 2 August 1939 Albert Einstein, who six years earlier had fled Nazi Germany to continue his research, wrote to President Franklin D. Roosevelt, informing him of a major development in his research which appeared to confirm the theoretical predictions of his famous Relativity Theory. Among its many radical ideas, it predicted that matter could be converted into energy and thus made into a bomb. Einstein's formula stated that: '$E = mc^2$ in which energy is put equal to mass multiplied by the square of the velocity of light showed that very small amounts of mass may be converted into a very large amount of energy.' Following the invasion of Poland during the following month, Einstein and another physicist, Leo Szilard, warned the US government of the peril that would threaten the world if Nazi Germany were allowed to win the race to produce an atomic bomb.

In 1941 an American committee reviewing atomic research carried out to date reported that it would take approximately four years to produce a nuclear explosive and that it would be eighteen months before a chain reaction in natural uranium was achieved. Furthermore, the committee estimated that it would take at least three to five years to produce sufficient weapons-grade uranium.

Five months after the United States' entry into the Second World War in December 1941, the decision was taken to proceed as quickly as possible with the Manhattan Project: the production of a nuclear weapon. In August 1942, the US Army was tasked with overall responsibility for the Manhattan Project and, in October, physicist Robert Oppenheimer was appointed as director of Project Y, the team of scientists who would design the actual bomb itself. During the 1920s, Oppenheimer had carried out research at the Cavendish Laboratory at Cambridge University, which was renowned for its pioneering work on atomic structure.

In 1943 the Manhattan Project's weapons division was established at Los Alamos, the site selected in November of the previous year by Robert Oppenheimer who had spent part of his childhood there. In the laboratory, Oppenheimer and his team carried out a programme of experiments with uranium and another radioactive material, plutonium.

Uranium is an abundant material which forms approximately two parts per million of the Earth's crust. Discovered in 1789 by Martin Heinrich Klaproth, who named it after the planet Uranus, it is the heaviest-known natural metal with a density of 19.04 gm/ml (that of lead is

11.34 gm/ml). It is a hard, dense element, silvery-white in colour, malleable and capable of being polished to a high degree although it tarnishes quickly on exposure to air.

Uranium ore is mined and then leached, subsequently being recovered by solvent extraction and roasting. This produces a crude concentrated material called 'yellow cake', which is dissolved in hot nitric acid, subsequently undergoing purification and calcination to form uranium trioxide. A further process of hydrogen reduction produces uranium dioxide, which can then be reduced further with calcium to produce metallic uranium in a powdered form. In order to produce metallic uranium, uranium dioxide is hydrofluorinated into UF_4 which is then mixed with magnesium metal filings and compressed before being baked at 900°C. A reaction between the UF_4 and the magnesium takes place, after which the molten uranium metal is poured into moulds.

Several types of uranium can undergo fission but uranium-235 does so more readily and emits a greater number of neutrons per fission than other such isotopes. A small amount of uranium in any assembly, known as a sub-critical mass, cannot undergo a chain reaction as neutrons released by fission are liable to leave without striking another nucleus and causing it to fission. If a further quantity is introduced, it increases the chance of released neutrons causing another fission as the latter are forced to traverse more uranium nuclei. There is a thus greater likelihood that a neutron will hit another nucleus and split it.

As we have seen in 'A Very British Bomb', plutonium is a synthetic element produced by irradiating non-fissile uranium-238 with neutrons. Fissionable, weapons-grade plutonium is plutonium-239, which has a critical mass only one-third of that of uranium-235. The element was first produced in mid-1941 at the University of California at Berkeley. It was already known, however, that the isotype plutonium-239 would be highly fissile.

As explained in 'A Very British Bomb', there are two methods of achieving an atomic explosion: the gun and implosion methods. By April 1945, it was recognized that sufficient uranium-235 would not be forthcoming for a test of a gun-assembly bomb until the beginning of August. However, there would be enough plutonium-239 for testing of an implosion-assembly device in early July and another in August.

The first plutonium test bomb, weighing 2 tons, was assembled at a solitary ranch house in New Mexico and on 14 July 1945 was hoisted to the top of a 30-metre (100-foot) high US Forest Service watchtower at a location known as the Trinity Site, 192 kilometres (120 miles) south of Albuquerque. In the early hours of 16 July a final warning flare was fired and at 5.29 a.m. the last firing circuit was connected and the bomb detonated. The energy yield of the explosion was equivalent to 21,000 tons of TNT. Such was the devastating sight and effect that Robert Oppenheimer was moved to quote the sacred Hindu text, the Bhagavad-Gita: 'I am become death, the shatterer of worlds.'

Three weeks later, at 8.15 a.m. on Monday 6 August, a single US Air Force bomber, a B-29 called the *Enola Gay*, flew over the Japanese city of Hiroshima and dropped a bomb, nicknamed 'Little Boy', of the untested gun-assembly uranium type. It exploded at an altitude of 580 metres (1,900 feet) over the city with the force of some 15 kilotons (15,000 tons of TNT), instantly causing appalling destruction to the surrounding area of 10 square kilometres (4 square miles).

About 66,000 people died instantly in the blast and a further 69,000 were injured. By the end of that year, the total loss of life in Hiroshima had risen to 140,000.

Three days later another B-29 bomber, *Bock's Car*, flew over the city of Kokura but bad visibility prevented the crew establishing the aim point. Flying on to Nagasaki, the aircraft dropped a plutonium bomb, nicknamed 'Fat Man', which exploded at 11.20 a.m. local time at a height of 500 metres (1,650 feet) with a force subsequently estimated to be equivalent to 21,000 tons of TNT. About 39,000 people were killed and 25,000 injured by the explosion, while almost half the city was destroyed. On 14 August, Japan surrendered.

Despite the end of the Second World War, the development of nuclear weapons continued with US scientists improving their efficiency and deadliness. The Americans decided, however, that they would keep their technology to themselves and, as recounted in the previous chapter, passed an Act of Congress outlawing any further disclosure of nuclear technology, even to the British who had been closely involved especially in the development of 'Fat Man'.

As already mentioned, the principal elements involved in the manufacture of nuclear weapons are plutonium-239 and uranium-235. The latter is, however, very costly and difficult to produce and for that reason plutonium-239 soon became the preferred element in the manufacture of nuclear weapons.

The heart of a nuclear bomb is known as a 'pit' (the American word for the stone in a peach or cherry) and comprises a sphere of fissile material (plutonium-239 or uranium-235) encased in a shell manufactured in a non-nuclear material such as stainless steel. During the functioning of a boosted nuclear weapon, a mixture of tritium and deuterium gas is injected into the sphere, which is then very tightly compressed by means of a high explosive, resulting in critical mass, and then energy being released by fission reactions.

Within a micro-second of detonation, the chain reaction causes the pressure inside the pit to reach millions of pounds per square centimetre and the temperature tens of millions of degrees. As the atoms split, energy is released in the form of X-rays that leave the bomb at the speed of light. The flash sets buildings, trees and people on fire before the explosion has even been heard. Air surrounding the bomb absorbs the X-rays and heats up, becoming visible. The huge increase in pressure creates a shockwave, which punches outwards from the centre of the explosion. Close behind are winds of over 480 kilometres per hour (300 miles per hour) which shatter and destroy everything within thousands of metres of 'ground zero'. A giant fireball of hot air begins to rise, sucking up thousands of tons of rock and earth while forming itself into the shape of a mushroom. The cloud will climb to over 15,000 metres (50,000 feet), a swirling mass of hot and highly dangerous radioactive particles – the fall-out. This will drift with the wind over thousands of kilometres before decaying and becoming extremely diffused.

Despite the United States' efforts at keeping the technology secret it was not long before it fell into the hands of the Soviet Union, whose physicists had been actively engaged in nuclear and atomic research during the 1930s. In February 1939 the Soviets discovered that the United States and Britain were researching the possibilities of nuclear fission, but any further Soviet research was terminated abruptly by the German invasion of Russia in June 1941. During early 1942 the absence of any articles on nuclear fusion or fission being published in western scientific journals, which had hitherto published them on a regular basis, heightened Soviet suspicion that the Allies were conducting secret nuclear research for military purposes. The physicist Georgy N. Flerov wrote to Joseph Stalin, urging that the Soviet Union should begin building an atomic bomb without delay.

During the following year, on the orders of Stalin, the Soviet nuclear physicist Igor Kurchatov, who had previously been the director of the nuclear physics laboratory at the Physico-Technical Institute in Leningrad, began a research project. By the end of 1944, some hundred scientists were working under Kurchatov. On 17 July 1945 Stalin attended the Potsdam Conference where he met other Allied leaders, including President Truman who commented to the Russian leader that the United States had just developed a 'new weapon of unusual destructive force'. On his return, Stalin ordered that work on the Soviet bomb project be stepped up. On 7 August, the day after the bombing of Hiroshima, he placed Lavrenty Beria, head of the NKVD, the Soviet secret police, in overall charge of it.

As described in 'A Very British Bomb', the Soviets had penetrated the wartime American nuclear weapons programme. On 29 August 1949, they carried out their first nuclear test of a bomb at Semipalatinsk, 2,880 kilometres (1,800 miles) south-east of Moscow. As already recounted, Britain followed suit on 3 October 1952. The global nuclear arms race had begun.

It was not long, however, before the United States and the Soviet Union achieved the next quantum leap in the development of nuclear weaponry: the thermonuclear or hydrogen bomb.

The principal difference between atomic and hydrogen bombs is essentially that of fission and fusion. In an atomic bomb, energy is released when heavy atomic nuclei (uranium-235 or plutonium-239) fissions. A hydrogen bomb utilizes the energy released when atomic nuclei of tritium and deuterium (isotopes of the light element hydrogen) fuse into heavier ones. A hydrogen bomb consists of two components: a primary (fission) and a secondary (fusion). The explosive process begins with the detonation of a fission bomb (the primary component); this creates the intense pressures and high temperatures (measuring several millions of degrees) that are necessary to set off the process of fusion in the secondary component. This entire process takes place within a fraction of a second.

A hydrogen or thermonuclear explosion is vastly more powerful than that generated by an atomic bomb. The blast effect is in the form of a shockwave that spreads outwards at supersonic speed, causing total destruction within a radius of several miles. The flash is of such an intense whiteness it can blind observers at a distance of several kilometres, while at the same time igniting fires. Fall-out contaminates the atmosphere, water and soil for many years. The explosive yield of thermonuclear weapons is also many times greater. While that of atomic bombs is calculated in kilotons, one kiloton being the equivalent of a thousand tons of TNT, the yield of thermonuclear devices is measured in megatons (equating to one million tons of TNT).

The first US thermonuclear bomb was tested on 1 November 1952 at Enewetak Atoll with the Soviet Union and Britain following in August 1953 and May 1957 respectively. China, which tested its first atomic bomb in 1964, carried out a thermonuclear test in 1967 while France, which had exploded its first atomic bomb in the Sahara in 1960, did likewise in 1968.

Such were the subsequent developments in thermonuclear weapons that within a decade the Soviet Union had exploded the largest bomb ever detonated on the face of this planet. It possessed 5,000 times the power of the bomb dropped on Hiroshima and its explosive yield was estimated to be the equivalent of 60 million tons of TNT. The power of a 60-megaton device is such that if dropped on a city anywhere in the world, it would destroy the entire city, most of the suburbs and start fires as far as 50 kilometres (30 miles) from the point of explosion, its fall-out meanwhile killing millions of people downwind.

The following years saw the deadly logic of MAD – Mutual Assured Destruction – with the superpowers realizing that none of them would start a war which none of them would win. Ironically, this proved to be one of the cornerstones of global peace as it ultimately led to negotiations over nuclear disarmament between the United States and the Soviet Union. The first tentative halt to the nuclear arms race came in 1963 with the Partial Test Ban Treaty. This was followed by the Strategic Arms Limitations Talks (SALT) which were initiated by President Lyndon B. Johnson in 1967 and ultimately resulted in the signing of the SALT I and SALT II agreements in 1972 and 1979 respectively.

The most important agreements within SALT I were the Treaty on Anti-Ballistic Missile (ABM) Systems and the Interim Agreement and Protocol on Limitation of Strategic Offensive Weapons. The ABM Systems treaty limited both the United States and the Soviet Union to one ABM launch site, and the number of interceptor missiles to 100, while the Interim Agreement and Protocol froze the numbers of intercontinental ballistic missiles (ICBMs) and submarine-launched ballistic missiles (SLBMs) to then current levels for a period of five years during which further negotiations for SALT II would be conducted. Both agreements were signed in Moscow on 26 May 1972 by Presidents Richard Nixon and Leonid Brezhnev. The ABM treaty was subsequently ratified by the US Senate on 3 August 1972.

Negotiations for SALT II lasted seven years, agreement being hindered by problems over asymmetry between US and Soviet strategic missile arsenals: the Soviet Union possessed missiles with large warheads while those of the United States were smaller but more accurate. Other problems relating to definitions, new developments and methods of verification also had to be resolved before final agreement could be reached. It was eventually signed on 18 June 1979 by President Jimmy Carter and Brezhnev, and submitted for ratification by the US Senate shortly afterwards, SALT II placed limits on a number of weapons systems: ICBMs and SLBMs which could be equipped with multiple independently targeted re-entry vehicles (MIRVs); long-range bombers capable of launching nuclear missiles; and strategic launchers. Each country was permitted a total of 2,400 systems.

During the following year, however, tensions between the United States and the Soviet Union, following the latter's invasion of Afghanistan in 1979, resulted in President Carter withdrawing the treaty from the Senate. Thereafter both sides observed the conditions of SALT II on a voluntary basis and in 1982 began further negotiations under the new heading of Strategic Arms Reduction Talks (START).

The purpose of START was to reduce the American and Soviet nuclear arsenals. Between 1983 and 1985, there was considerable interruption. In 1985, however, negotiations were resumed and in July 1991 an agreement was reached under which the Soviet Union would reduce its total number of warheads from 11,000 to 8,000 with the United States reducing its stocks from 12,000 to 10,000. Reductions were also made in both sides' numbers of ICBMs, SLBMs, long-range bombers and mobile launchers. In May 1992, following the collapse of the Soviet Union, the United States conducted negotiations separately with the former Soviet states of Russia, Belarus, Ukraine and Kazakhstan. This led to an additional agreement under which all sides would adhere to the terms of the 1991 START treaty and the latter three states would either destroy all their nuclear weapons or deliver them to Russia.

In 1991 the United States and Russia began dismantling their nuclear arsenals. Between them, they agreed to destroy over 50,000 nuclear weapons. The destruction process started off with much publicity, the world's media watching as missiles and bombs were fed into massive hydraulic presses and crushers or packed with high explosives and blown up. In reality, however, what the television cameras were recording was merely the destruction of empty casings; there was no mention of what was happening to the plutonium 'pits'. The truth is that these were posing a major unforeseen problem with regard to disposal.

When plutonium was first produced in the United States for use in nuclear warheads, little or no thought was given to the ultimate problem of its disposal when such weapons were dismantled at the end of their operational lives. In the words of Victor Rezendes, Director of Energy and Science at the General Accounting Office, 'From day one when we first produced plutonium in this country, we never had an option for its disposal. The notion always was that we were at war, the production of nuclear warheads was the key and the most paramount thing for this country to achieve. The disposal option was always considered something that would be done down the road.'

While US scientists were rather belatedly turning their attention to this problem, heavily guarded convoys of vehicles carrying nuclear weapons were already heading for central Texas from missile bases throughout the United States. Their destination was, and continues to be, a massive nuclear storage depot at Pantex, outside Amarillo. For over forty years, Pantex had been the final assembly centre for the majority of the United States' nuclear weapons. Now its products, unused and no longer required, were returning to be dismantled.

Operated by the US Department of Energy, it is America's only nuclear weapons assembly and disassembly facility and as such is probably the most secure and heavily guarded installation in the world. Located on the high plains of the Texas Panhandle, 27 kilometres (17 miles) north-east of Amarillo, it occupies a 16,000-acre site just north of Highway 60 in Carson County. Originally constructed in 1942 by the US Army Ordnance Corps for the loading of artillery shells and bombs, it was converted in 1950 for nuclear weapons assembly, testing, quality assurance and repair. Ultimately, its operations were extended to include disassembly, retirement and disposal of nuclear weapons, fabrication of chemical high explosives and high-explosive development work in support of research establishments. Currently, Pantex's task is to dismantle between 1,500 and 2,000 nuclear weapons per year.

Those entering or leaving the complex are searched thoroughly by heavily armed guards. Closed-circuit television cameras maintain constant surveillance around its perimeter and throughout the different sectors comprising the entire installation. Ground radar and seismographic detectors pick up anything moving around the perimeter, even Texas jackrabbits attempting to burrow under the razor-wire fences. Throughout the sensitive areas of the installation, tall poles are sited to prevent unauthorized helicopters from landing while armoured vehicles, equipped with machine-guns, patrol the nuclear storage areas.

On arrival at Pantex, nuclear warheads are taken to deep within the installation where they are unloaded and moved to a transit area. There they are subjected to a detailed check: scanning for any damage, cracking or corrosion and ensuring that their safety mechanisms have not been tripped. If no problems are found, the weapons are moved to massive blast-protected bunkers, nicknamed 'Gravel Gerties', for dismantling.

All weapons are first stripped down to their constituent parts, which total some 6,000 in all. The highly complex arming mechanisms are then removed; in the case of bombs this is followed by the parachute assembly which is designed to allow a delivering aircraft the chance to fly well clear as the bomb descends to the predesignated height at which it will explode. Finally the 'physics package', containing the plutonium warhead, and its high-explosive casing, is swiftly removed from the remainder of the weapon and transferred immediately to high-security areas within the installation.

More sophisticated weapons such as Tomahawk cruise missile nuclear warheads are subjected to further tests. Inside their steel casings, the warheads are surrounded by highly radioactive tritium gas which is used as the booster necessary to produce the fusion explosion. Any leakage of the gas would be extremely dangerous; to test it for such, each warhead is placed in a powerful vacuum chamber. As the air in this is pumped out to within a few millionths of an atmosphere, the pressure differential will force the gas to leak from even the most microscopic cracks and be detected.

Gold and silver connectors are extracted from warhead assemblies for recycling, while all plastic and metal components are removed and crushed before being placed in permanent storage as low-level radioactive waste. The plutonium pit in each weapon is, however, left intact. Indeed it cannot be crushed, burned or destroyed in any way as no technology exists for its disposal. There is no alternative but for it to be placed in highly secure storage.

Each 'pit' is placed inside a steel barrel fitted with a cellulose fibre liner and sealed. Barrels are then stored above ground in concrete bunkers originally constructed to store conventional munitions during the Second World War. They are stacked in racks by a sophisticated hydraulic loader specially designed to protect the operator, each barrel then being bar-coded. Thereafter, laser readers travel up and down along the rows of stacks, checking that the correct numbers of barrels are still in place and that there are no excessively high radiation readings which would indicate damage to any of them. Forty-ton concrete blocks are positioned in front of the bunkers' doors to secure them. The pits are currently destined to remain sealed inside their barrels stored in the bunkers for the foreseeable future. It was expected that by the year 2000, 20,000 pits would be in storage – each one more powerful than the bombs dropped on Japan in 1945.

Pantex has, however, experienced problems over transportation of weapons to the installation and suffered an escape of tritium gas from a bomb. In addition, a nuclear weapon was accidentally dropped while being dismantled. The result of all these problems was a scaling-back of the rate at which warheads were being dismantled and consequently during one year only 63 per cent of the target figure for that period was achieved.

Contamination of the seventeen US Department of Energy installations that have been involved in the dismantling of nuclear warheads also poses a major problem. Initially gauged at tens of billions of dollars, the estimated cost for decontamination was subsequently put at 300 billion dollars – a figure now thought to be probably too low. Indeed, it is almost impossible to arrive at a firm figure as the technologies necessary for decontamination do not exist. Some of the installations will thus remain contaminated for centuries.

As described earlier, plutonium was first produced in 1941 as a by-product of uranium. As with all radioactive materials, it has a 'half-life' which is defined as the period of time required for half a gram (a fiftieth of an ounce) of radioactive material to decay completely to the point of being totally harmless. All the plutonium on this planet is approximately fifty years old but its half-life is over 24,000 years. Total decay will take over 250,000 years.

The principal problem with plutonium is the emission of an alpha particle which is a helium nucleus. Very heavy and slow moving, it does not easily penetrate other materials: a layer of dead skin cells will stop an alpha particle. While plutonium outside the human body is thus not a major concern, it becomes one if ingested or inhaled, because the alpha particle causes ionization of cells in the body which can mutate into cancerous forms and other materials. Tests have shown that only eighty-millionths of a gram of plutonium is required to cause cancer.

There are an estimated 200 to 250 tons of plutonium either in nuclear warheads or removed from them. In addition, there are approximately 1,000 tons of highly enriched uranium associated with nuclear weapons worldwide. As large numbers of missiles and bombs are dismantled, the problem facing governments and scientists is the long-term disposal of the highly enriched uranium and plutonium extracted from them.

There are four optional means for disposal of such materials. First, recycling for use in nuclear fuel – a method advocated by many people. Second, vitrification and burial in specially constructed storage areas. Third, transmutation into isotopes which cannot be used in the manufacture of weapons. Last, send the material into space and dump it in the sun.

While the West regards plutonium extracted from weapons as waste and concerns itself with developing disposal technology, Russia takes a different viewpoint, regarding it as a fuel for use in the generation of nuclear power. Minute quantities of weapons-grade plutonium are mixed with low-grade uranium to produce a fuel called mixed uranium–plutonium dioxide (MOX) which is used in pellet form in fast-neutron breeder reactors. This is, however, a difficult and costly procedure and would require massive investment on the part of the Russians to enable them to convert their reactors to use MOX. Furthermore, it would not dispose of the plutonium completely as the spent fuel would have to be reprocessed when extracted from the reactors – the remaining plutonium would have to be removed, mixed with uranium and then returned to the reactor as MOX once again. Thus the MOX elements would have to be recycled a large number of times in order to dispose of the plutonium, making this impractical as a single-cycle method of disposal.

If the sole criterion is the prevention of plutonium being used in the manufacture of weapons, the most favoured method of disposal is vitrification, which is already used in the disposal of high-level waste from nuclear reactors. The plutonium is contaminated with radioactive poisons to prevent any attempt to recover it in the future and then fused with silica to produce molten borosilicate glass which is sealed into steel canisters. Each canister is rigorously checked for leakage by remote-controlled probes before being moved to a permanent storage area. However, this method has only been used for the disposal of reactor waste and so far no one has been able to vitrify weapons-grade plutonium successfully. When and if they succeed in doing so the material will have to be interred for 250,000 years in a highly secure site. Furthermore, those responsible for doing so will have to be certain that the material encasing the poisoned plutonium does not deteriorate and eventually fall away, leaving an accumulating deposit of pure plutonium.

The option of transmutation has also been given serious consideration. In the mid-1990s, research began on the use of linear accelerators to destroy plutonium. The process would involve taking hydrogen atoms (comprising protons with electrons spinning round them) and stripping off the electrons. The protons are fired into a linear accelerator and their positive charge pushes them forward on the front of an electric field, in a similar fashion to a surfer riding a wave. By the time they reach a point three-quarters of the way down the accelerator's tube, the protons have accelerated to almost the speed of light. At the far end of the tube they smash into a block of lead, producing a shower of neutrons that are absorbed into the plutonium which breaks up into short-lived, more stable elements. The results of initial experiments looked promising, but at the time even the most optimistic forecasters estimated that it would be a minimum of fifteen years before transmutation of plutonium by linear acceleration would be a viable proposition.

Meanwhile, research was also conducted into the final option of launching consignments of plutonium into space and dumping them in the sun. Consideration had to be given to the possibility of launch failures and the risk of a massive catastrophe involving a cargo of several tons of plutonium. Research was carried out into the development of crash-proof containers capable of withstanding impacts at the highest velocities possible according to the laws of physics. Like transmutation, however, it is a long way from being a viable process.

In the meantime, plutonium pits continue to be stored in barrels in the absence of any international policy for their disposal. Under the terms of the SALT II agreement of June 1979, limiting the numbers of intercontinental ballistic missiles, submarine-launched ballistic missiles, heavy bombers and strategic launchers, the total number of warheads in the United States and Russia was restricted by the year 2003 to no more than 3,500 each, of which 1,750 could be deployed on submarines. Although SALT II was never ratified, due to renewed tensions between the two countries following the Soviet Union's invasion of Afghanistan, its arms limitations were observed voluntarily by both countries. During the 1980s the nuclear arsenals of the United States and the Soviet Union exceeded the SALT II limits by a factor of ten, thus posing a massive problem of disposal requiring colossal expenditure. In 1994 it was estimated that the cost of dismantling one nuclear warhead was between 30,000 and 100,000 dollars, with tens of thousands waiting to be dismantled.

While the United States could afford to devote considerable resources to dismantling its nuclear weapons, this was not the case with Russia and the former Eastern Bloc countries which were suffering, and continue to do so, from unstable economies and a lack of hard currency. Evidence of the lack of funding for the Russian nuclear industry could be seen in the virtually unguarded and heavily contaminated radioactive waste sites outside Murmansk, the nuclear reactors badly in need of repairs and modernization and a nuclear ballistic missile submarine lying on the bed of the Barents Sea with its warheads still aboard.

In 1991, as the Soviet Union began to disintegrate, senior figures in the Russian political and military establishments became concerned over the threat to the security of the vast quantities of nuclear weapons located throughout Russia and what were fast becoming former Soviet states. They turned to the United States and in particular to two members of the US Senate, Senators Sam Nunn and Richard Lugar, requesting their assistance in safeguarding Russia's nuclear arsenal.

While Nunn and Lugar were receptive to the Russians' approach, recognizing the dangers posed by the risk of nuclear weapons falling into the wrong hands, the same could not be said for the rest of the US political establishment and the country as a whole. The United States was understandably glad to see the end of the forty-five-year-long Cold War which had cost it dear, and was reluctant to commit itself to large-scale assistance to its old foe. Indeed, the House of Representatives had already thrown out a proposal for financial assistance to the tune of one billion dollars for the former Soviet Union. Furthermore, 1991 was a presidential election year and the presidential candidates, George Bush and Bill Clinton, were concentrating their attentions on vote-winning domestic rather than foreign issues.

Despite the odds stacked against them, however, Nunn and Lugar took up the challenge and succeeded in winning other members of the Senate to their cause, developing a plan for the collaborative dismantling of the former Soviet nuclear arsenal. Remarkably, they succeeded and in November 1991 the Co-operative Threat Reduction (CTR) Program, also known as the Nunn–Lugar Program, was passed by the Senate, subsequently being approved by the House of Representatives and signed off by President George Bush.

The CTR Program had five objectives. First, it was to assist Russia in carrying out reduction of its strategic arms to levels in accordance with the terms of the START treaty; this was to be carried out with the establishment of weapon dismantling and destruction projects. Second, it was to assist in reduction and prevent proliferation of nuclear weapons and fissile material by enhancing the safety, security, centralization and control of nuclear weapons throughout the former Soviet Union; the dismantling of weapons would result in large quantities of fissile material which would thereafter have to be securely stored and controlled. Third, assistance was to be given to Kazakhstan and Ukraine in the elimination of weapons and delivery systems infrastructures to be limited under START; this would entail establishment of facilities for dismantling missiles, silos, heavy bombers and their weapons.

The Program's fourth objective was to assist the former states of the Soviet Union to eliminate and prevent proliferation of biological and chemical weapons by helping them to achieve compliance in accordance with the 1993 Chemical Weapons Convention; this would involve the elimination of a biological weapon production facility in Kazakhstan and provision of assistance to Russia in the destruction of its chemical weapon stocks as well as the elimination of its production facilities. The CTR Program's final objective was to promote demilitarization and military reform throughout the new states of the former Soviet Union, assisting the armed forces of each state in their transition to western lines, as well as to reduce proliferation threats by providing assistance for improvement of border security and controls designed to prevent illicit movement of material and technology related to nuclear, biological and chemical weapons.

Initial progress was slow, primarily because of Russian reluctance or refusal to allow access to nuclear facilities and because it took time before sufficient funds became available; but by the following year the Program was gaining momentum. A number of major engineering projects were established in Kazakhstan, Belarus, the Ukraine and Russia with American companies carried out the task of dismantling weapons and delivery systems. Among the latter were well-known names such as Hewlett Packard, Raytheon, Lockheed-Martin, Westinghouse, Bechtel, Allied Signal, AT&T and Caterpillar.

In June 1996 the Ukraine was declared totally free of nuclear weapons. A special facility had been built for the dismantling of missiles, with warheads being removed and missiles extracted from silos after which they were broken up. The silos themselves were then blown up and the entire area ploughed and turned over to agriculture. A total of 111 SS-19 Stiletto lightweight ICBMs were dismantled, 144 SS-19 silos were destroyed and 1,900 nuclear warheads were returned to Russia. Fifty-five SS-24 medium ICBMs and fifty-one silos were also destroyed, their 460 warheads having been removed beforehand and deactivated. The CTR Program also provided for the building of 261 houses at the Pervomaysk ICBM base and 605 apartments at the Khmelnitsky as part of the demobilization of six regiments of the Strategic Rocket Forces of the former Soviet Union.

In addition, a number of Tu-95 Bear and Tu-160 Blackjack long-range bombers were also dismantled, the latter being a variable-geometry aircraft of similar appearance to the US Air Force's B-1 bomber but larger. With a range of 14,000 kilometres (8,700 miles), the Blackjack could carry up to twelve Kh-55MS (NATO designation AS-15 Kent) cruise missiles, each of which carried a 200-kiloton nuclear warhead and had a range of 3,000 kilometres (1,865 miles).

In November, Kazakhstan also became completely rid of nuclear weapons by the CTR Program: 104 SS-18 Satan heavy ICBMs and 1,400 nuclear warheads had been returned to Russia. Produced in six variants (Models 1 to 6), each with a differing warhead configuration, the SS-18 was the largest missile in the Soviet armoury and indeed in the world, having a maximum range of 16,000 kilometres (nearly 10,000 miles). The highly accurate Model 4 was capable of carrying up to ten multiple independently targeted re-entry vehicle (MIRV) 500-kiloton warheads. With a further 204 being stationed in Russia, it was estimated that the Model 4 force alone had the capability of destroying 65 to 80 per cent of the United States' ICBM silos, using two warheads against each.

In addition, 147 (mostly SS-18) silo launchers, missile control centres and test silos at Zhanghiz-Tobe, Derzhavinsk, Semipalatinsk and Leninsk were dismantled and destroyed. Meanwhile, thirteen vertical test boreholes at the Soviet nuclear weapons test facilities at Balapan were sealed; in the Degelen Mountains, a massive complex of 181 test tunnels and shafts was also closed and sealed.

Besides large numbers of missiles, Kazakhstan also held a huge amount of weapons-grade uranium produced for use as fuel for a new type of submarine developed by the former Red Navy. The uranium, in the form of fuel pellets, had been produced at the Ulba Metallurgical Plant at Ust-Kamenogorsk. The development programme had proved a failure and had been abandoned, but by that time a vast amount of uranium fuel had been produced. No longer required, it was consigned to the vaults of the plant and forgotten. In 1992, following the creation of the Republic of Kazakhstan, the existence of the fuel came to light and the Kazakh government turned to the Americans. An initial investigation by the US team revealed a quantity of just over a thousand containers of uranium-235 enriched to 90 per cent – sufficient to manufacture fifty nuclear weapons. Aware that countries such as Iraq and Iran would be keen to acquire the fuel for use in their own nuclear weapons development programmes, the Americans decided to move quickly.

On 8 October 1994 a highly sensitive operation, code-named Project Sapphire, was launched. Three giant C-5 Galaxy transports of the US Air Force flew a team of thirty-one specialists and 130 tons of equipment, including a mobile nuclear laboratory, to Ust-Kamenogorsk. Here, 600 kilograms (1,320 pounds) of uranium-235 were stored and there was concern that it might be stolen. During the following six weeks, the team packed and sealed the uranium in special stainless-steel containers. In addition, it packed some 30 kilograms (66 pounds) of uranium oxide powder, a quantity of spent fuel rods and other material. By the time the task was complete, the entire consignment comprised fifty steel drums ready for shipment by air to the United States. On 20 November the team, accompanied by the uranium, flew back to the United States where the entire consignment was transported to the US Department of Energy's Y-12 plant at Oakridge in Tennessee.

The United States took similar measures three years later when the former Soviet state of Moldavia announced that, because of its parlous financial situation, it was putting up for sale twenty-one of its air force's MiG-29 Fulcrums, of which fourteen were Fulcrum-C variants capable of carrying nuclear weapons. This caused considerable anxiety in Washington, where there were fears that nations such as Iran might attempt to acquire the aircraft and thus a nuclear delivery capability. Furthermore, the US Air Force was keen to lay its hands on the Fulcrum-C in order to discover more about it and, in particular, its helmet-mounted display system and AA-11 Archer air-to-air missiles. In June 1997, a deal was struck between Moldavia and the United States, the latter purchasing 500 AA-11 missiles and a large quantity of spares in addition to the twenty-one aircraft. In October, a fleet of US Air Force C-17 Globemaster transports flew the Fulcrums, missiles and spares from Moldavia to Wright Patterson Air Force Base in Ohio.

In Belarus, meanwhile, a total of eighty-one SS-25 Sickle lightweight mobile ICBMs, together with all the infrastructure for their support and maintenance, were removed to Russia and the country was declared free of nuclear weapons in November 1996. However, any further work under the CTR Program was terminated as a result of gross violations of human rights by the tyrannical regime of Belarus's Communist dictator, President Alexander Lukashenko, who had come to power in 1994.

It was in Russia, however, that the CTR Program carried out the majority of its work and is continuing to do so. A high priority was the collection from throughout the former Soviet Union of some 30,000 tactical nuclear weapons. Another was the destruction of SS-18 Satan ICBMs, these posing the foremost threat to the United States. Under the terms of the START II Treaty, missiles equipped with MIRV warheads were banned. Russia was required to reduce its arsenal of SS-18s by a total of 254 by the beginning of 2003 and the CTR Program became heavily involved in assisting in carrying out that requirement: destroying rocket motors, providing facilities for the disposal of rocket fuel, dismantling warheads and storing fissile material. During the period up to December 1999, 116 SS-18s, 119 SS-11 Sego, ten SS-17 Spanker, thirteen SS-19 and thirty submarine-launched ballistic missiles (SLBMs) were destroyed, along with fifty missile silos and forty-two heavy bombers. In addition, 100,000 tons of missile liquid propellant were also eliminated.

Dismantling of warheads obviously raised the question of secure storage of fissile material. Existing Russian facilities, inadequately guarded and possessing little in the way of security systems, were totally unsatisfactory. Consequently, in October 1992, the United States signed an agreement with Russia for the design and construction of the Fissile Material Storage Facility, half of the cost of the facility being borne by the United States. Designed by the US Corps of Engineers, it was originally intended to be located at Tomsk but was eventually sited at Mayak in Siberia, just over 1,280 kilometres (800 miles) east of Moscow. This was also the site of the designated RT-1 nuclear reprocessing plant. Construction began in the autumn of 1994 and the first stage of the facility is due for completion in 2002; it will accommodate plutonium removed from over 6,000 weapons.

In addition, the United States supplied over 26,000 fissile material containers for use at Mayak; 117 railcar conversion kits to enhance rail transport of nuclear weapons; 150 containers and 4,000 Kevlar ballistic blankets for security and ballistic protection of nuclear weapons during transit; emergency support equipment (including five mobile response complexes) in case of accidents involving nuclear weapons; and computer systems and training to enhance Russian capability for accounting and tracking of nuclear warheads.

Checks to ensure that CTR Program assistance is being used properly are carried out through a system of audits and examinations (A&E). During October 1999, a total of seventy-six A&Es were carried out in Russia, Ukraine, Kazakhstan and Belarus, evaluating assistance which had been provided at a cost of 599 million dollars out of the total of 2.1 billion dollars allocated to the CTR Program. Detailed reports on the results of these audits are submitted to the US government and Congress.

A major area of concern was the large number of nuclear submarines and other vessels lying inactive since the demise of the Soviet Union. In October 1996 a report in the British *Daily Telegraph* described fifty-two decommissioned nuclear submarines of Russia's Northern Fleet rotting at anchor off the Kola Peninsula, among them seventeen Victor and November Class vessels laid up at the remote naval base of Gremikha in the eastern part of the peninsula, and others at the Sevmorput naval yards at Murmansk and Polyarny. In March 2000 a report by the Bellona Foundation, the Norwegian organization established in 1986 to monitor nuclear safety issues related to the former Soviet Union military complex, was published in its *Nuclear Chronicle*. The report quoted the Russian Ministry of Nuclear Energy (Minatom) as stating that thirty first- and second-generation Northern Fleet vessels, all of them still containing spent fuel, were in danger of sinking and that leakage from the primary cooling circuits in their reactors had been detected. Having been moored for up to fifteen years, their hulls were badly corroded and were no longer watertight. Similar problems were also reported to exist at several naval bases and yards belonging to the Pacific Fleet.

While such vessels may no longer constitute a military threat, they pose a major one to the environment. As stated by the Bellona Foundation in a report in August 1998, the submarine branch of the Soviet/Russian Navy has had a chequered history with regard to nuclear safety. Between 1961 and 1998, there were several accidents on submarines in which a total of over 500 people died, the most serious being caused by fires or severe damage to nuclear reactors through cores overheating, with release of radioactivity occurring in some cases. In three instances, the accidents were so severe that the vessels sank; all of them involved submarines of the Northern Fleet. One of these took place in

October 1986 in the Atlantic Ocean, north of Bermuda, when the Yankee Class submarine K-219 suffered an explosion in one of her missile tubes, possibly following a collision with an American submarine. The vessel was forced to surface after a fire broke out in the missile compartment and water starting leaking into the vessel. Eventually, the crew had to abandon ship and she subsequently sank, her two reactors and sixteen missiles ultimately posing a hazard to the environment.

The most publicized accident involving a Soviet submarine took place in the Barents Sea 480 kilometres (300 miles) off the coast of Norway, west of Bear Island. On 7 April 1989 the Red Navy Mike Class submarine K-278 *Komsomolets* suffered a fire that broke out in her stern and spread to other compartments. The 6,400-ton vessel, the sole forerunner of a new class, possessed a titanium hull designed to enable her to operate at depths of 1,000 metres (3,280 feet),and was equipped with an advanced type of reactor that propelled her at speeds faster than those of any other submarines in existence. The *Komsomolets* surfaced but the internal pressure caused by the fire and high-pressurized oxygen resulted in her hull rupturing and she sank to the seabed 1,685 metres (5,528 feet) below, with the loss of forty-two lives, including that of her commander.

Initially, it was considered that the wreck posed only a small threat to the marine environment surrounding it but during the following years a report stated that there was a risk of leakage by 1995 from the reactor and two R-84 nuclear torpedoes, containing a total of 4 kilograms (9 pounds) of plutonium, with which the vessel was armed in addition to her conventional weapons. According to a subsequent Norwegian report, the motor of one of the R-84s had been damaged in the accident and leaked fuel which, on making contact with salt water, had produced ammonia. There was a danger of the gas reacting with other fuel aboard the sunken vessel and causing an explosion. In the summer of 1994, an expedition was carried out to survey the wreck and seal off the areas of high risk. Signs of plutonium leakage were detected and it was discovered that one of the R-84 warheads had broken open and released 22 grams (about 1 ounce) of plutonium. The expedition succeeded, however, in plugging some of the holes in the submarine's hull.

Although the subsequent levels of radioactivity emanating from the *Komsomolets* were low, Norwegian scientists were concerned by plankton and other organisms consumed by fish becoming contaminated and entering the food chain. Fishing had to be cut back in the area due to minor contamination levels and the perceived threat of further, more extensive contamination. This in turn had a major effect on Norway's fishing industry; its revenues from sales of fish to Europe and Russia were threatened.

Three options were considered for resolving the problem of the *Komsomolets*. The first, that of raising the entire vessel, was soon dismissed as being too hazardous as well as costing in the region of an estimated 1 billion dollars. The second option was to raise the bow section containing the two R-84 torpedoes; this was also rejected as being too dangerous since it was considered that leakage could have rendered the weapons unstable. The third and most feasible option was to hermetically seal the entire submarine in a gel, manufactured from the shells of crustaceans and containing 2 per cent chitosan, which would, it was envisaged, bind radionuclides more efficiently than concrete. This would, however, be only an interim measure as eventually the warheads would have to be removed due to the plutonium-239 in them having a half-life of 24,000 years. The sealing of the submarine was scheduled for the summer of 1995 and, according to the Bellona Foundation, took place at some point thereafter.

A total of some 250 nuclear-powered submarines were built by the Soviet Union; by the time of writing, in mid-2000, 183 of them, from both the Northern and Pacific Fleets, have been laid up for one or more of three reasons: in accordance with START treaty requirements, the vessel's age or lack of facilities for proper repair and maintenance. Of those, 120 still contain spent fuel in their reactors. The Russian Navy does not possess the proper infrastructure nor facilities onshore for the removal of spent fuel from its submarines. Instead, it uses a fleet of twelve tankers and a further twelve ships and barges to transport and store spent fuel and liquid radioactive waste. Most of the tankers are, however, over twenty-five years old and the majority of the other support vessels are no longer in a functional state and were themselves due for decommissioning by the end of the 1990s.

Their desperate state was illustrated during 1999 when two incidents took place involving vessels of the Pacific Fleet. In August, there was a leak of liquid radioactive waste aboard a support tanker based at the Zvezda shipyard in the city of Bol'shoy Kamen; in December, one of the Pacific Fleet's four ageing storage barges caught fire while loaded with 100 submarine spent fuel assemblies. In order to improve the situation in the Northern Fleet, eight nuclear-powered icebreakers operated by a civilian organization, the Murmansk Shipping Company, from its Atomflot base at Murmansk, were pressed into service as support vessels.

Following the collapse of the Soviet Union, the increased decommissioning of submarines inevitably exacerbated the problems of storage and ultimate disposal of radioactive waste and spent nuclear fuel. Lacking the necessary infrastructure and facilities, Russian efforts at storage were makeshift, spent fuel being stored in the reactors of decommissioned vessels and ashore in obsolete storage facilities and transport containers. At the end of February 1999 the Bellona Foundation reported in *The Nuclear Chronicle* that the most dangerous site was at Andreeva Bay in the Kola Peninsula, 64 kilometres (40 miles) from the border with Norway, where 21,000 spent fuel assemblies were stored in containers outdoors.

The report also mentioned that similar situations existed at the Gremikha naval base and at the Pacific Fleet base at Shkotovo. According to a report by Igor Kudrik in *The Nuclear Chronicle*, by the year 2000 the Russian Navy would be storing almost 105,000 spent fuel assemblies from its Northern and Pacific Fleets, these representing between 228 and 238 submarine loads as each vessel was equipped with two reactors, each containing 220 to 230 fuel assemblies. In addition, the Murmansk Shipping Company is currently storing 3,500 spent fuel assemblies, removed from its eight icebreakers, while the Northern Fleet is doing likewise with seven submarine reactor cores. None of these can be reprocessed in the normal way by the RT-1 plant at Mayak: the fuel assemblies are of a zirconium-coated type and the cores are from Alpha Class submarines which were equipped with liquid metal cooled reactors. A further 3,130 zirconium-clad spent fuel assemblies are also stored in the support vessel *Lotta* moored at Atomflot icebreaker base at Murmansk.

A further problem exists at Murmansk where a nuclear cargo vessel, the *Lepse*, is also moored at the Atomflot base. During the period 1962 to 1981, the vessel was used as a support ship for the Murmansk Shipping Company's ice-breakers. Since 1981, however, it has been used as a floating store for 624 spent fuel assemblies, some of which are damaged with the fuel jammed inside, salvaged after an accident aboard the icebreaker *Lenin*, the remainder being from Northern Fleet submarines. Some of the assemblies are zirconium-clad and cannot be reprocessed at Mayak's RT-1 plant.

In 1992 the CTR Program initiated a further programme for dismantling nuclear ballistic missile submarines as required by the terms of the START I treaty. Four locations were initially considered for the work to be carried out: Nerpa in the Kola Peninsula, Zvezdochka in Archangel County (south-east of the peninsula), Zvezda in the far east of Russia and the nuclear reprocessing plant at Mayak. In 1996, after a further review of the project, the decision was taken to construct special dismantling facilities at Nerpa and Zvezdochka.

During 1997, however, it became apparent that the Russian government was unable to pay the shipyards to carry out the dismantling work. The CTR Program therefore contracted directly with the shipyards and in 1999 signed contracts for dismantling seven vessels: one Yankee and six Delta class strategic ballistic missile submarines (SSBNs). Of those, one was already dismantled, three had spent fuel removed and the remaining three were defuelled during 1999 in accordance with the contracts.

At the time of writing, the immediate objective of CTR's submarine dismantling programme was the destruction of a total of thirty-one SSBNs: one Yankee, twenty-six Deltas and five Typhoons. The destruction of the latter will remove a major threat to the United States. Powered by four pressurized water-cooled nuclear reactors, the Red Navy's six Typhoons are the largest underwater vessels ever constructed with each carrying twenty SS-N-20 Sturgeon submarine-launched ballistic missiles (SLBMs), each equipped with ten MIRV 100-kiloton warheads. The SS-N-20 has a range of 8,300 kilometres (5,160 miles) which would have allowed a Typhoon to fire its missiles from within the Arctic Circle and hit targets anywhere within continental United States.

The submarine-dismantling aspect of the CTR Program was initially concerned only with the destruction of SSBNs, with priority being given to relatively new vessels. During 1997, however, the Russians raised the subject of general purpose nuclear-powered submarines. In Russian naval vernacular, the term 'general purpose' would normally cover submarines armed with torpedoes, depth charges and anti-ship cruise missiles. In the context of nonproliferation and disarmament, however, the Russians applied it to all laid-up or decommissioned submarines not covered by the CTR Program.

By 2000, some 110 such vessels will have been laid up, comprising submarines of the Alpha, Charlie, Echo, Hotel, November and Victor classes. In February 1999, an official of the US Department of Energy stated that the United States would be launching a programme for the dismantling of general-purpose submarines once cost and project assessments had been made. In a speech given in December 1999 at a conference at the Centre for Nonproliferation Studies at the Monterey Institute of International Studies, Senator Richard

Lugar emphasized the importance of the destruction of the cruise-missile-equipped vessels once the dismantling of ballistic missile submarines was complete. If funding is granted by Congress, this additional part of the submarine-dismantling program may begin during the period 2002 to 2003.

Measures have also been initiated for dealing with the problem of spent fuel. The Arctic Military Environmental Co-operation (AMEC) organization, established in 1996 by the United States, Norway and Russia with the role of focusing on environmental hazards posed by military activities in the Arctic, designed and built a 40-ton steel–concrete cask, with an operating life of fifty years, for local storage and transportation of spent fuel assemblies. In 1998, US Vice Secretary of State Strobe Talbot announced a project to design and construct fifty giant 80-ton casks, but such is their size and weight that there have been misgivings over the manageability of such containers.

According to a report by the Bellona Foundation, however, around 430 of the AMEC 40-ton flasks would be required to defuel a total of some 150 laid-up submarines, ninety of them currently moored at different locations in the Kola Peninsula. The use of casks, however, is only a partial solution to the storage problem as sites for them have not yet been prepared. A number of locations at Andreeva Bay, Gremikha, the Nerpa shipyard and the Kamtchka Peninsula in the far east of Russia are under consideration but no firm decision has been made to date. Furthermore, problems have arisen in the form of a dispute with the Russian State Nuclear Regulator (GAN) which, according to the Bellona Foundation, has refused to license the casks, claiming that production models would not be manufactured to the same standards as the prototype which passed all the GAN tests. These criteria included drop-tests and exposure to fire and water, designed to ensure that the spent fuel in six containers inside the cask remained intact.

It appears that part of the problem lies in the long-running dispute between the Defence Ministry and GAN: the latter for many years has been attempting to gain control of naval nuclear sites such as the nuclear waste facilities in the Kola Peninsula. At the same time Minatom has entered the fray by trying to strip GAN of any influence on matters concerning nuclear safety at Minatom and Defence Ministry sites. A total of 100 casks were due to be manufactured at a plant at Izhora, near St Petersburg, at a unit cost of 150,000 dollars, with the CTR Program bearing the cost of the first twelve casks. Should GAN be proved correct in its allegations over production standards, the CTR Program would be forced to cancel its order, although Minatom has already stated that in such circumstances it would pay for the casks. Nevertheless, the dispute has highlighted the safety issues surrounding spent fuel, and the problems facing western organizations and governments that wish to have the question of liability settled in order that they are not made responsible for any damage caused by a nuclear accident involving any equipment manufactured or financed by them.

September 1998 saw the completion of a liquid waste processing facility at the Atomflot base at Murmansk. The project, established in 1994 by the United States, Russia and Norway, upgraded existing facilities, increasing capacity from 1,200 cubic metres (1,570 cubic yards) of liquid radioactive waste per annum to 5,000 cubic metres (6,540 cubic yards). The facility was designed to handle not only the waste generated by the Murmansk Shipping Company's eight icebreakers but also all that produced by the Northern Fleet's warships.

Other international projects to solve the problems caused by dismantling submarines have included the funding by Japan of a liquid radioactive waste processing facility for the Pacific Fleet in the Russian far east. Designed by the American company Babcock & Wilcox, it was constructed at the Amur shipyard and subsequently tested at Vostok before entering service at the Zvezda shipyard in late 1998. Like the AMEC casks, however, the project has encountered problems, with the Russians now maintaining that it would be too expensive to operate and that it would be unable to cope with the quantities of waste produced.

Under the auspices of the Commonwealth of Independent States Co-operation Programme (CISCO), the European Union has also participated in a number of projects dealing with the potential environmental hazards, caused by pollution from nuclear spent fuel and radioactive waste. Apart from several regional studies, it has been involved in two specific projects. The first of these was a feasibility study into the removal and subsequent management of the 624 spent fuel assemblies currently stored in highly unsatisfactory conditions aboard the support vessel *Lepse*. The other project was a feasibility study into the options for storing large amounts of spent fuel at the RT-1 processing plant at Mayak. Unfortunately, however, the Russians dismissed the findings, which showed that the cost of a new dry storage facility would be less than that of upgrading the existing wet storage on which construction had ceased several years previously.

Norway has been involved in the majority of projects and has played a leading role in putting forward a number of initiatives. These comprise emptying and closing the spent fuel storage facility at Andreeva Bay; carrying out a study for the management of the fuel and the construction and operation of a facility for temporary storage; establishment of a temporary spent-fuel storage facility at Mayak; construction and operation of a specialist vessel for transportation of spent fuel; construction and operation of four special railcars for transportation of spent fuel; the upgrading and operation of a temporary spent fuel storage facility at the Zvezdochka shipyard in Sverodvinsk; delivery of a mobile liquid radioactive waste treatment facility for use at Murmansk; resolving the problems caused by the support vessel *Lepse*; and upgrading the radioactive liquid waste treatment facility at the Atomflot base at Murmansk.

International efforts aimed at resolving the major potential environmental hazards have, however, been hindered by a number of obstacles within Russia itself. Contributing nations naturally required certain safeguards, similar to those that protect the CTR Program, before they were prepared to release funds for projects. Among these were ratification by the Russians of taxation and customs exemptions, as well as nuclear liability agreements. In addition, they needed a plan from the Russians as to how they intended to deal with the whole question of management, storage and disposal of radioactive material. Finally, there was the problem of obtaining access for international experts to sites at which projects would take place. Solutions to all these problems were slow in appearing although there has reportedly been progress in the last year or so.

The situation has not been improved by a recent chilling in relations between the United States and Russia, caused by a growing disparity in power as Russia became increasingly reliant financially on the West. The situation was exacerbated by other factors, including Russia's financial collapse in 1998, Bosnia, the crisis in Kosovo, the enlargement of the North Atlantic Treaty Organisation (NATO), corruption scandals in Russia itself and the war in Chechnya, where the West became increasingly concerned at the scorched-earth tactics adopted by Russian forces.

While the CTR Program has succeeded in reducing the threat of nuclear conflict through the destruction of strategic weapons and delivery systems in accordance with the terms of the START treaty, the threat of proliferation still remains. As described in the next chapter, countries such as Iran and Iraq are currently seeking to develop their own military nuclear capability by attempting to obtain materials and technology from within the former Soviet Union.

RUSSIAN
ROULETTE

The end of the Cold War saw a rapid deterioration in the former Soviet Union's arsenal, which rapidly fell into disrepair. Ironically, this resulted in a greater risk than ever of missiles being launched, not as an act of war but either by accident or without authority.

Just after dawn on 25 January 1995, the world came closer to a nuclear holocaust than at any time since the Cuban missile crisis of 1962. A Russian radar early-warning station in the Kola Peninsula detected a swiftly moving object, measured at over 1,500 kilometres per hour (932 miles per hour), approaching north Russian airspace from the direction of the Barents Sea, an area always treated very seriously by the Russians as US Navy strategic ballistic missile submarines (SSBNs) were known to operate there. During the following five minutes there was mounting alarm as the operators at the radar station flashed details of the fast-approaching threat up the chain of command to a senior officer on duty, via a special terminal system called 'Krokus', stating that they suspected it to be a missile from an American submarine. They were under considerable pressure: seven years earlier a young German, Matthias Rust, flying a light aircraft, had penetrated Soviet air defences and landed in Moscow's Red Square. There had been severe repercussions and so on this occasion the radar operators, despite fearing a reprimand for sounding a false alarm, were concerned to avoid suffering the same fate as their predecessors.

Doubtless thinking along the same lines, the senior officer, a general, decided that it would be prudent to pass on the alert to higher levels rather than subsequently be held responsible for initiating a catastrophic holocaust. He transmitted it via 'Kavkaz', a complex system comprising cables, radio links, satellites and relays that represented the heart of the Russian command and control system. Kavkaz communicated the alert to three portable command and communications systems called 'Chegets'; these are contained in three briefcases that at all times accompany the Russian President, the Defence Minister and the Chief of the General Staff. Similar in principle to the nuclear 'football' that permanently accompanies the President of the United States, the Chegets allow instant communication between the three leaders and the General Staff's national command centre. President Boris Yeltsin, Defence Minister Pavel Grachev and the Chief of the General Staff, General Mikhail Kolesnikov, were soon in communication.

Meanwhile, the radar operators reported that the object was separating and immediately it was assumed to be a Trident II D-5 SLBM deploying its MIRV warheads. Certainly, it appeared to be displaying the characteristics of the much-feared American missile, which can carry up to eight W-76 or W-88 warheads with explosive yields of 100 kilotons or 475 kilotons respectively.

Orders were flashed to the command posts of Russia's Strategic Rocket Forces, ordering them to go to a state of increased readiness to launch; at the same time, similar orders were also transmitted to the commanders of the Russian Navy's ballistic missile submarine fleet. At that time, despite the end of the Cold War and the deterioration in her armed forces, Russia still maintained forty-five strategic ballistic missile submarines. During the next four minutes, commanders waited for the next order in the sequence which would lead to their missiles being launched but, eight minutes after the alarm was first raised, the objects faded from Russian radar screens as they fell into the sea; a major crisis had been averted.

The incident had been caused by the launching of a Norwegian rocket as part of a scientific research programme into the Northern Lights. As the elements of the rocket's first stage had fallen away, they had resembled Trident SLBM MIRV warheads heading south into Russian territory. The Russians had, however, been warned of the launching beforehand. On 21 December 1994, the Norwegian Foreign Ministry had sent a letter to neighbouring countries and the Russian Foreign Ministry, advising that between 15 January and 15 February Norway would be launching a Black Brant XII, a four-stage research rocket as part of a collaborative project with the US National Aeronautical and Space Administration (NASA), the latter having supplied the engines.

The issuing of such a warning letter was a familiar procedure for the Norwegians, who had launched 607 rockets since 1962. On this occasion, however, the letter had become lost in the slow-moving bureaucratic system of the Russian Foreign Ministry. An official had taken down the details but for some unexplained reason the information had not been passed on to the Defence Ministry and ultimately to the forces manning Russia's early-warning system. This oversight, however, was just one factor that had caused the crisis. There was a much larger, more fundamental reason.

During the forty-five years of the Cold War, the Soviet Union expended vast resources in a massive defence programme under which it amassed a huge arsenal of nuclear weapons totalling in 1991 an estimated 11,159 warheads. As part of a massive military infrastructure which covered the Eastern Bloc, the Soviets established a two-tier early-warning system known as 'Kazbek' and comprising seven ground-based Dnestr and Dnepr 'Hen House' radars which provided total coverage of the airspace around Soviet territory.

In 1982, nine military satellites were launched to detect launches of US land-based ICBMs: these were positioned in high-elliptical orbit, looking down at an angle and searching for infra-red emissions that would signal the heat of missile exhausts. The satellites were, however, inclined to stray from orbit and had to be replaced frequently. The system was designed with a certain amount of built-in redundancy, seven satellites being sufficient to cover the entire United States. Information on any launch would have been transmitted down to a network of radar vessels, constantly criss-crossing the oceans and seas on the Earth's surface, which would in turn have relayed it to the headquarters of the General Staff in Moscow.

During the late 1980s a second system, comprising four satellites in geostationary orbit, was also deployed. Its exact role has never been ascertained but it is thought to have been tasked with covering gaps in the coverage of the nine high-elliptical orbit satellites. The geostationary satellites' ability to cover the oceans patrolled by American and British SSBNs has never been confirmed but Paul Podvig, of the Center for Arms Control, Energy and Environmental Studies in Washington, believes that at least one of them, Cosmos-2224, is able to do so. But despite the addition of the geostationary satellites gaps still remained. During every twenty-four hours the high-elliptical orbit system was blind for two periods of six hours and one hour respectively. Even with the assistance of one of the geostationary satellites, there was still a period of three hours each day when there was no Soviet satellite surveillance at all.

This highly sophisticated early-warning system, however, fell into disrepair during the 1990s with the radars, which had been built in the 1960s and 1970s, reaching the end of their operational lives by the late 1990s. They were due to be replaced by 'Daryl' and 'Volga' type radars with further early-warning stations being constructed to ensure 360° coverage of Soviet airspace. Two-thirds of the construction of the new stations had been finished by the early 1990s but the subsequent collapse of the Soviet Union not only prevented the work being finished but also left some of the radars outside Russia in newly independent states which no longer wished to accommodate them: at Mykolayiv in the Ukraine; at Mingacevir in Azerbaijan and at Balqash in Kazakhstan. One of the key locations was in Latvia from where it covered the areas over the North Atlantic and North Sea where American and British SSBNs were believed to be on patrol. In May 1995, however, following their independence from the Russian Federation, the Latvians destroyed a newly constructed radar station, thus opening a gap in radar coverage to the west only partially covered by satellites, a number of which had ceased to function; by 1999 only three high-elliptical orbit and two geostationary satellites were still operational. Another radar station was built in Belarus to compensate for the one lost in Latvia, being completed in late 1998 and early 1999.

Partially blind, the Russians were thus forced to assemble a relatively primitive backup system which provided far less accurate data. In addition to some of the satellites no longer being operational, most of the radar ships were decommissioned. Such were the gaps in coverage that in 1999 American researchers were able to map 'corridors' from the Pacific and the Far East along which missiles could be launched into the heart of Russia.

The fact that Russia's nuclear deterrent force now depends on an unreliable early-warning system has very serious ramifications given that Russia still maintains its Cold War era policy of 'launch-on-warning': launching its missiles when those of the enemy are still airborne. This policy was originally designed to prevent the former Soviet Union's nuclear weapons being destroyed by a pre-emptive strike. Russia currently relies heavily on launch-on-warning because of the high level of vulnerability of its forces. Due to lack of resources to keep their strategic nuclear forces at a constant state of high readiness, the Russians can no longer disperse their mobile and submarine-launched nuclear weapons into forests and oceans. Currently, only one or two of the Russian Navy's SSBNs are deployed at sea at any given time and perhaps only one regiment of nine mobile missiles is dispersed from its base. Consequently, the bulk of the Russian nuclear arsenal is based in its silos, parked in its peacetime bases or moored in naval docks where it is very vulnerable.

While it may have been valid during the Cold War, during which the Kazbek system was functioning efficiently, the launch-on-warning policy is now highly dangerous and the consequences could be nothing short of catastrophic, leading to the destruction of major urban centres in other nuclear powers such as the United States, Britain, France and China. One typical Russian missile, such as the SS-18 Satan ICBM or SS-N-20 SLBM, reportedly would cause at least ten times the devastation of the bomb dropped on Hiroshima in 1945.

Such is the risk of a missile launch resulting from a wrongly identified threat that the West has been forced to take the problem very seriously, despite most Russian military analysts claiming that the chances of such an occurrence are very slim. This is based on the premise that Russia's 3,000 remaining nuclear missiles and launch systems are equipped with safety systems to prevent a mistaken launch. According to these analysts, no Strategic Rocket Forces missile could be launched without the receipt of special codes transmitted by the National Command Authority.

Authority to launch is transmitted via the Cheget briefcase systems accompanying the Russian President, the Defence Minister and the Chief of the General Staff who are the three individuals responsible for making the decision to launch Russian missiles and who as the official holders carry the key to each case. Each Cheget case will respond only to the handprint of its respective official holder who must enter his own password before the system can be activated. Once access is granted, contact is established with the General Staff command centre. Using the integral telephone, each of the three official holders can communicate with military advisers. Any degree of launch can be ordered, ranging from a single missile to an all-out nuclear strike. Once it has been agreed between the President, the Defence Minister and the Chief of the General Staff, the authorization code is transmitted by the national command centre. The order to launch cannot be transmitted from one of the cases alone; it must be confirmed by the other two.

The Cheget system is designed to provide a guarantee against an accidental launch or one based on mistaken data, while at the same time reducing delays in launch authorization to a minimum. It was introduced in 1983 following the deployment of American SSBNs equipped with the Trident I C-4 SLBM in Norwegian waters in 1979. With a Trident taking only ten minutes to reach Moscow, as opposed to the thirty-minute flight time of an ICBM launched in the United States, Soviet leaders needed to be able to respond to a threat more swiftly than had previously been the case.

The requirement for such a rapid-response communication system was highlighted in 1983 when, at just past midnight on 26 September, alert alarms sounded in a secret bunker at Serpukhov-15, the strategic nuclear weapons command bunker from which the Soviet Union monitored its high-elliptical orbit satellites watching US land-based ICBMs. In command of the bunker that night was Lieutenant Colonel Stanislav Petrov. As he sat in the commander's chair, one of the satellites reported that a nuclear missile attack was under way; the computer analysed the information and indicated that five Minuteman ICBMs had been launched from their silos in the United States. Petrov reported the alert to his superiors at the early-warning system's headquarters; they in turn passed it to the General Staff's national command centre which was responsible for contacting the Soviet leader, Yuri Andropov, and with whom the latter would consult concerning the launch of a retaliatory attack.

Fortunately, Lieutenant Colonel Petrov chose to disbelieve the information, deciding that it was a false alarm and advising his superiors as such. His decision was based on the fact that there was no indication of any threat from the Kazbek early-warning system's radar stations, which were controlled from a different command centre; furthermore, having previously been told that a nuclear attack would be massive, he guessed that any American attack would have involved a far larger number of missiles. His decision resulted in a nuclear holocaust being avoided but his subsequent treatment at the hands of his superiors did not reflect any recognition of that. Following the incident he was investigated and questioned at length, his interrogators unsuccessfully attempting to make him a scapegoat. Although he was not punished for his actions that night, neither was he rewarded; he eventually retired to life as a pensioner living outside Moscow.

The false alarm was subsequently traced to one of the satellites which had picked up the sun's reflection off some clouds and had interpreted it as a missile launch. The incident was particularly dangerous as it took place during a period of tension between the Soviet Union and the United States; only a few weeks earlier, Soviet aircraft had shot down the Korean Air Lines Flight 007. It was later described by a former CIA analyst, Peter Pry, as 'probably the single most dangerous incident in the 1980s'.

In the eyes of the Russians, American and British SSBNs still pose a threat and thus they have retained the Kazbek system. In the event of an attack a ten-minute countdown would begin, during which Russian political and military leaders would have to determine how to respond. At every stage, stringent safeguards are supposed to be in place to prevent a mistake or a bad decision made under pressure.

At nine minutes to impact, operators in the radar early-warning centre try to confirm that blips on their screens are missiles. At eight minutes, contact is established with senior officers at the national command centre who activate the three Chegets, alerting the three official holders. A minute later, the three leaders are in contact with the radar early-warning centre, confirming that an attack is in progress, and discuss what action should be taken. At six minutes, the special communication circuit is switched on, connecting the headquarters of Strategic Rocket Force formations with regiments equipped with silo-based missiles as well as others with mobile missile launchers and missile-carrying trains. At the same time, commanders of Russia's Northern and Pacific Fleets are also alerted and order the commanders of their SSBNs to go to a state of immediate readiness.

By five minutes, the three Russian leaders will have had to come to a decision and transmitted their orders to the national command centre, which in turn transmits the unblocking codes to missile and submarine commanders. At three minutes to impact, missiles are prepared for launch. Under the safety procedures, officers in the field or at sea must confirm that the orders received by them are genuine. At two minutes, missile commanders use keys to activate their missile systems and enter the unblocking codes. At one minute to impact, they await the final orders. If it does not arrive, the missiles will not be launched. If it does, firing buttons are pressed.

The safety procedures carried out at every stage are designed to prevent an unauthorized or mistaken launch but there is now evidence that the chain of command can be circumvented. According to one report, Strategic Rocket Force commanders have stated that it is now possible for a junior officer to launch a missile without authorization from the national command centre.

As recounted in the previous chapter, since the collapse of the Soviet Union and the breaking away of some independent states, all nuclear weapons previously based in the Ukraine, Kazakhstan, Belarus and other states were withdrawn to Russia where they were stored at locations all over the country. Some have since been dismantled and destroyed under the auspices of the Co-operative Threat Reduction Program but, according to official figures released on 30 July 1999, Russia still possesses a large number of strategic nuclear weapons comprising just over 7,000 warheads carried by ICBMs of the Strategic Rocket Forces, SLBMs of the Russian Navy and bombers of the Russian Air Force. In addition, it possesses between 6,000 and 10,000 tactical nuclear weapons.

During the Cold War, the Strategic Rocket Forces were considered the premier service in the Soviet Union. Originally formed in 1946 as a special purpose brigade of the Supreme High Command Reserve, in 1960 they were designated the 24th Guards Division of the Strategic Rocket Forces (Raketnyye Voyska Strategicheskogo Naznacheniya – RVSN). On 7 May 1960 the RVSN was elevated to the status of an armed service in their own right, on a par with the other four Soviet armed services: the Army, Navy, Air Force and Air Defence Forces. All strategic nuclear missiles with a range of over 1,000 kilometres (621 miles) were thereafter assigned to the RVSN while tactical nuclear weapons remained the responsibility of the Army, Navy and Air Force. By 1962, the year of the Cuban missile crisis, the

RVSN comprised 110,000 men and, as the Soviet Union continued its massive programme of nuclear weapon development in its efforts to seek parity with the United States, thereafter expanded further. By the early 1970s, the Soviet Union had achieved superiority in numbers of nuclear weapons, by which time the RVSN numbered some 350,000 men.

Control of all RVSN formations was, and continues to be, exercised directly by the Supreme Commander-in-Chief via the national command centre of the General Staff and the RVSN's own main headquarters, using a multi-level network of command posts on twenty-four-hour monitoring watch. Twelve thousand personnel are responsible for maintaining weapons and communications systems in a fully operational state and, in the event of an alert, reacting instantly by bringing missiles to an immediate state of readiness for launching.

The aftermath of the collapse of the Soviet Union, however, has seen large-scale deterioration in the majority of the Russian armed forces. While the RVSN is still supposed to be first and foremost among the Russian armed forces, it has nevertheless suffered. Previously, officers and soldiers were well paid and such was the standing of the RVSN, based on the importance of their role, that their commander-in-chief took precedence over his counterparts in the other four armed services. The situation is now very different. Officers often go without pay for many months and when it is received, it is pitifully low. Like the rest of the Russian armed forces, budgets within the RVSN are tight and bills frequently go unpaid; it is common for the heating in missile bases to be switched off, requiring personnel to work in very low temperatures. At some bases, the underground command posts are crumbling and suffer from flooding. Many soldiers have been forced to moonlight as taxi drivers and, in extreme circumstances, to beg. In some instances, officers in the RVSN have vented their anger by going on strike. In the late 1990s, the ever-increasing degree of hardship resulted in suicide rates increasing throughout the Russian Army to unprecedented heights.

According to Dr James Thompson, a psychologist at University College London who has spent several years investigating the effects of low morale in the Russian armed forces, 'You have to work in the hope that everyone else is going to do their job properly and that you'll be paid at the end and there's someone evaluating your progress, to praise you when you do well. When that breaks down, people tend to go into their own little groups, with their own agendas. They will see what they can get away with, in testing the system. You will believe that no one is going to inspect you, if you fool around. Nuclear weapons and people have always been a bad mix, but when those people haven't been paid, are badly managed and are within a system which has totally lost morale, then there is a danger of unauthorized actions and indeed, those could culminate in an unauthorized launch.'

Further problems have been caused by RVSN units being understrength. With a current total strength of some 100,000, of which 50,000 are conscripts, the RVSN is at approximately 85 per cent of its establishment. This has resulted in officers of all ranks having to carry out spells on alert duty more frequently, on average a total of 130 twenty-four-hour periods per year. Of RVSN officers, 99 per cent have a degree in engineering and over 25 per cent of non-commissioned personnel are volunteers; the remainder are conscripts carrying out two years' service, more than half of whom have no secondary education.

One of those who has dared to voice his concern over the deteriorating situation is Colonel Robert Bykov, a former officer in the RVSN who has become increasingly anxious about the lack of safeguards for launching missiles of which he has extensive knowledge. During the 1960s he was involved in developing and improving them, carrying out tests in remote areas of Siberia. Currently semi-retired, he now investigates problems within the RVSN and his findings have made him very unpopular, so much so that he fears for his life and with good reason – in 1994 an attempt was made on it. After receiving a tip-off that some secret documents had been left in a briefcase, he arranged to meet two other officers and a close friend, a journalist named Dima Kholodov, at the location where the briefcase had been left for them. Kholodov arrived before the others and opened the briefcase. Unfortunately, it contained a bomb which exploded, killing the journalist; the principal suspects were believed to be RVSN officers who resented Bykov's team investigating their affairs. Since then Bykov, who has continued his investigations, has lived behind steel doors at his apartment and has tried to stay out of trouble.

Such was his concern over the current state of the RVSN, however, that Bykov continued to speak out. In 1997, he wrote an article published in a Russian newspaper, *Komsomolskaya Pravda*, in which he disclosed that Russia's nuclear forces were in danger of falling apart, stating that equipment and systems frequently ceased to operate properly and that the central command systems could no longer be relied upon, periodically going into 'loss of regime mode' in which it would refuse to transmit commands. Even more worryingly, he also revealed that there had been reports of individual missile silo systems switching automatically to combat mode, although he maintained that the main command system would prevent an accidental launch. Following the publication of his article, Bykov was investigated by the Federal Security Service.

Bykov's article had repeated similar claims made shortly beforehand by Defence Minister General Igor Rodionov. In January 1997, increasingly concerned at the continuing disintegration of Russia's strategic nuclear forces, he attempted to contact President Boris Yeltsin, but he was ill and unable to see Radionov. He resorted to writing a letter, voicing his anxiety and informing the President that command and control systems, including the early-warning system and the underground command posts, were disintegrating. He advised Yeltsin that the reliability of the control systems could no longer be guaranteed and that the situation might soon be reached whereby Russian nuclear weapons could no longer be controlled. When Rodionov was finally granted an interview with Yeltsin, he was rebuked for writing the letter.

Almost immediately afterwards, Rodionov was dismissed and replaced by General Igor Sergeyev, commander of the RVSN, who subsequently acknowledged that the command and control systems were ageing and that the RVSN was suffering major problems, including shortages of trained manpower and lack of housing for up to 17,000 of its officers.

During the heyday of the Soviet Union, the RVSN always enjoyed top priority in terms of funding and personnel. With the arrival of Mikhail Gorbachev, however, funds for maintenance and upgrading were slashed drastically and inevitably equipment and systems suffered as a result. Ageing computers developed faults and began to malfunction. The command, control and communications network was beyond its intended lifespan and was in desperate need of overhauling and replacement. There were reports of an increasing frequency of false signals transmitted for no apparent reason, playing havoc with the computer systems.

As mentioned earlier, there were also incidents of highly automated systems switching to combat mode of their own volition within a matter of seconds, behaving as though they had received launch orders and beginning to execute programmes leading to the firing of weapons. Fortunately, no missile has so far accidentally entered the final stage of combat mode; the absence of the unblocking codes transmitted from Moscow system was designed to prevent this happening. Those codes are required to permit activation of switches which complete launch circuits.

Colonel Robert Bykov maintains, however, that the system is far from foolproof and that bored operators have interfered with the safeguards. Having studied the launch systems, they have become totally familiar with them to the extent that they discovered aspects of which even the designers were unaware. By rewiring the circuits, they were able to circumvent the key switches and complete the launch circuits. Consequently, there have reportedly been instances where some officers could feasibly have carried out unauthorized launches.

According to Bruce Blair, a former officer in the American nuclear forces and now an academic at the Brookings Institution in Washington specializing in research on Russian nuclear weapons, this is entirely possible. 'There are ways to circumvent safeguards; the question is: how much time and impunity are offered to an aberrant unit to do these sorts of things? I'm reminded of the situation in Ukraine which essentially could have taken control over strategic missiles based on its territory and, by the Russian General Staff's own estimation, bypassed the existing locking devices, the safeguards on those missiles, within a matter of days to weeks. So clearly, all of these safeguards only work for a period of time.'

In 1996 the Russian Defence Ministry formed a department to investigate any instances of troops discovered to be tampering with missile launch circuit systems. The ministry's principal concern was that if a missile was launched, there was no way it could be destroyed or rerouted in mid-flight. In order to reduce the risk of an unauthorized launch, the ministry imposed an additional safeguard whereby at least two, in some instances three, men were required to launch a missile. Two separate keys had to be turned before the firing button was pressed. According to Robert Bykov, however, this measure proved ineffective in practice. If one man was asleep or left his position, the remaining man could easily operate the system and carry out an unauthorized launch.

In 1994 Russia, the United States and Britain took the major step of detargeting their ICBMs and SLBMs. Missile computers were given a new programme, the Zero Program. If any missile was launched accidentally or without authorization, it would land in the middle of the sea. At least, that was the theory. According to Bruce Blair, the detargeting agreement was entirely cosmetic and symbolic, and had absolutely no effect on the combat readiness of Russian and US forces. Nor did it reduce the risk of unauthorized or accidental use of nuclear weapons.

The truth is that original programmes, containing Cold War targeting co-ordinates, have remained in Russian missile system computers. In the event of a member of the RVSN deciding to launch a missile without authorization, the system can be switched from the Zero Program to the Cold War targets within seconds. Some Russian military analysts fear it may even switch of its own accord. According to Alexander Pikayev, a member of the defence committee of the Duma, Russia's lower house of parliament, irrespective of whether or not a launch is authorized, if a missile is launched the computers would switch from the Zero Program to the Cold War target co-ordinates and thus the weapon would fly against its targets anyway.

In 1997, however, it became apparent that an even more serious threat exists in the form of a device which is potentially far more dangerous than any strategic or tactical nuclear weapon. During the Cold War, both the Soviet Union and the United States developed Special Atomic Demolition Munitions (SADM) for use by special forces. In essence these were miniature thermonuclear bombs, each comprising a plutonium core surrounded by high explosive which, when exploded, as described in 'Dismantling the Bomb', produces an extreme and uniform increase in pressure leading to a nuclear explosion.

In the case of the American device, the W-54 Special Atomic Demolition Munition, it was developed between 1960 and 1963 and some 300 were deployed from 1964 until 1988. Based on the W-54 warhead, it had a variable explosive yield of 0.01 to one kiloton. This was the same warhead as used in the Davy Crockett tactical nuclear weapon system which used a 120-mm or 155-mm recoilless rifle to launch a nuclear projectile designed for use against Soviet troop formations. Weighing just over 23 kilogrammes (51 pounds), the W-54 was the smallest and lightest implosion-type fission bomb ever deployed by the United States. Designed for sabotage attacks against enemy command centres and strategically vital points on lines of communications, such as bridges, tunnels, and dams, the W-54 SADM weighed less than 74 kilograms (163 pounds) and was carried in a special case containing the cylindrical warhead, a code-decoder and firing unit. A larger unit, the Medium Atomic Demolition Munition (MADM), was also developed; weighing less than 182 kilograms (400 pounds), it was in service from 1965 to 1986.

The W-54 SADM's Soviet counterpart reportedly had an explosive yield of one kiloton, sufficient to devastate part of a city and kill up to 50,000 people. If such a device was detonated in the centre of London, for example, it would destroy all buildings within a 500-metre (1,640-foot) radius, killing up to 20,000 people within that area. Up to a radius of one kilometre, there would be more destruction and approximately 50 per cent casualties. Within hours, prevailing winds would carry nuclear fall-out as far as the M25 motorway, requiring London to be evacuated. Unlike the W-54 SADM, the Soviet model was built into a briefcase and, activated by a key, incorporated a timer that could be set for periods from under an hour to several days.

In May 1997 General Alexander Lebed, Russia's former Security Council Secretary, paid a visit to Washington. During a closed meeting with Congressman Curt Weldon, Chairman of the House of Representatives' National Security Committee, he disclosed that eighty-four of 132

SADM-type weapons could not be accounted for by the Russian Defence Ministry. In September, during an interview broadcast on the American television programme *60 Minutes*, and on another with the Russian news agency Interfax, he stated that special atomic demolition munitions had been produced for use by Spetsnaz troops of the Main Intelligence Directorate (GRU) of the General Staff and that he had first been made aware of their existence during his period of tenure as Secretary of Russia's Security Council. Lebed concluded by stating that such weapons, possessing no safety systems of the type incorporated into other tactical nuclear weapons, were ideal for use by terrorists.

Lebed's statement about the existence of Russian SADMs was immediately dismissed by Moscow, which had always denied the existence of such devices, stating that all Russian nuclear weapons were strictly accounted for and stored under the tightest possible security. US State Department officials meanwhile adopted a similarly sceptical attitude, stating that there was no evidence to support Lebed's claims.

Days after Lebed's revelations Vladimir Denisov, who had served as his deputy on the Security Council, suggested during an interview with Interfax on 13 September that all tactical nuclear weapons such as SADMs had been withdrawn to central storage facilities while adding, 'It was impossible to say the same about former Soviet military units which remained on the territory of the other states in the CIS.' He also stated that, 'There was no certainty that no low-yield nuclear ammunition remained on the territory of Ukraine, Georgia or Baltic States or that such weapons had not appeared in Chechnya.' This appeared to support a remark made by Lebed in one of his interviews to the effect that the majority of the GRU's Spetsnaz units were deployed along the former Soviet Union's borders and thus some SADMs may have remained in former Soviet states after the USSR's collapse.

On 22 September, Lebed received support from Professor Alexei Yablokov, a former adviser to President Boris Yeltsin on environmental affairs, who published a letter in the newspaper *Novaya Gazeta* confirming the existence of the SADMs, which by this time were being popularly referred to as 'suitcase bombs', and stating that he had met the scientists who had designed them.

Two days later, however, the newspaper *Pravda* published an article in which a spokesman for Minatom dismissed both Lebed's and Yablokov's claims, repeating earlier government statements that all Russian nuclear weapons were stored under strict control. On 25 September Lieutenant General Igor Valynkin, chief of the Defence Ministry's Twelfth Main Directorate (which, better known as the Twelfth GUMO, is the organization responsible for the storage and security of all tactical and strategic nuclear weapons), also publicly refuted Lebed's and Yablokov's claims. In an interview with journalists, he claimed that all Russian tactical nuclear weapons had been withdrawn to special central storage sites controlled by the Twelfth GUMO to ensure that they did not fall into the hands of terrorists. Valynkin went on to admit that it was technically possible to produce a miniature warhead but denied that the Soviet Union or Russia had ever produced such a device.

Further denials of the existence of such weapons followed from other Russian government departments, including the External Intelligence Service (Sluzhba

Vneshney Razvedki – SVR) which succeeded the KGB's First Chief Directorate, all of whom denied any knowledge of such devices. The head of the National Centre for the Reduction of Nuclear Danger, Lieutenant General Vyacheslav Romanov, also added his voice in denying the existence of such weapons, as did General Lebed's successor as Security Council Secretary, Ivan Rybkin, who stated that no documents relating to SADMs had been found in the council's records.

All such denials were, however, largely undermined on 27 September by a programme broadcast by the ORT television network which recounted how small nuclear devices, with yields ranging from 0.01 to 0.35 kilotons, had been manufactured for geological and oil exploration purposes, and had been used in Kazakhstan during the mid-1970s. In addition, the programme revealed that small nuclear weapons had also been developed for military use but had been returned to Russia in the early 1990s.

On 6 October, General Lebed repeated his claims at an international conference in Berlin, stating that he believed that SADMs had been manufactured in the Soviet Union and that he had been unable to investigate the locations of those missing before being dismissed. On that same day, however, President Yeltsin signed a number of amendments to the Russian Federation Law on State Secrets, classifying all information concerning military nuclear facilities. On 31 October, Professor Alexei Yablokov publicly threatened to release details of the nuclear 'suitcases' unless the President replied to a letter that he had sent him four days earlier.

At the beginning of November, the Kremlin implicitly admitted that SADMs did exist and it was subsequently revealed that in 1996 General Lebed, appointed Security

Council Secretary by President Boris Yeltsin after withdrawing his challenge to the latter for the presidency, had indeed been tasked with mounting an investigation into the number of such weapons manufactured and their whereabouts. A special commission had been formed on 23 July 1996 to check whether such weapons were in the Russian Army's nuclear arsenal, interview any specialist troops trained in their use, and investigate whether similar weapons could be manufactured illegally. Headed by Vladimir Denisov, it included representatives of Minatom and the Russian security services, and by September had reached the conclusion that no SADMs were stored in Russian Army arsenals. Lebed's report, submitted to President Yeltsin, had confirmed the existence of such weapons and stated that only forty-eight of them were accounted for. He had not, however, had the opportunity to pursue his investigations further. On 18 October, both he and Denisov had been ousted from the Security Council and no efforts had been made to investigate further the matter of the missing SADMs.

On 6 November, following the Kremlin's admission, Professor Alexei Yablokov was summoned by the Russian Defence Council and co-opted to draft a presidential decree co-ordinating efforts to locate all 'compact nuclear weapons', bring them under secure control and arrange for their subsequent destruction as soon as possible. Not only was this a further tacit admission that the weapons existed; it also confirmed that they were not under secure controls and thus could be a major security risk.

Meanwhile, following his dismissal by President Yeltsin as Secretary of the Security Council, General Lebed had left Moscow for Krasnoyarsk, a huge province in Siberia, where he was subsequently elected governor. In April, when interviewed for this programme, he was asked to confirm that eighty-four SADMs were missing. Refusing to talk while being filmed, he subsequently revealed off-camera that his public statement about the missing SADMs had led to his being investigated by Russia's State Prosecutor for alleged disclosure of state secrets; if he was found guilty, it would be the end of his political career and thus any further comments made by him would only reinforce the case against him. When Congressman Weldon was interviewed in May 1998, he was quite clear about what Lebed had said to him in 1997: 'He said his job was to account for 132, as the Chief Adviser for Defence to Boris Yeltsin. He said he could only find forty-eight. We were startled. We said, "General, what do you mean you can only find forty-eight?" He said, "That's all we could locate, we don't know what the status of the other devices were, we just could not locate them."'

In September 1998, further confirmation of the existence of the Russian SADMs came when a former colonel in the GRU, the highest-ranking officer ever to defect from the organization, testified in closed hearings before the US Congress. During his testimony, he reportedly stated that he personally had identified and reconnoitred locations for the emplacement of SADMs to be used in the event of war. While he had no knowledge of any of the weapons having been smuggled into the United States, he conceded that it was possible given that a number of them had disappeared from Russia's inventory of tactical nuclear weapons. The colonel reportedly revealed that the weapons could be armed only by trained specialists, the process taking some thirty minutes, and that they would self-destruct if opened improperly. He also disclosed that the SADMs would have been smuggled into the United States in a similar fashion to drugs, by light aircraft or boat, or landed on the coast by submarine. Members of GRU Spetsnaz units would have retrieved them and subsequently concealed them close to their intended targets, one such location being the Shenandoah valley in northern Virginia, only a short distance from Washington. The colonel reportedly also disclosed that during the 1962 missile crisis, SADMs had been stockpiled in Cuba without the knowledge of the Cubans.

During 1999 there was considerable further speculation over the allegedly missing SADMs but no definitive information on their whereabouts. In his interview in May 1998, Congressman Curt Weldon also recounted details of a meeting in December 1997 with Defence Minister General Igor Sergeyev: 'I went to Russia on my thirteenth trip out of fourteen or fifteen that I've taken, last December, and I requested, besides my other meetings, a meeting with the Defence Minister ... And I said to General Sergeyev, after a wide range of topics that we discussed in a session that lasted well over an hour, I asked him specifically: "One, did you build small atomic demolition munitions, as we suspect you did? Two, do you know where they are? And three, have you destroyed them all?" And to me he said, "Yes, we did build them, we are in the process of destroying them, and by the year 2000 we will have destroyed all of our small atomic demolition devices, the so-called nuclear suitcases."'

As Congressman Weldon went on to point out, while he believed General Sergeyev to be sincere, there was no proof that the Russians had in fact located all the SADMs that had been built: 'The key question is not just to make sure that they're destroyed but were there others? Are there others that have not been accounted for? Perhaps not just to the Ministry of Defence, perhaps built by the Ministry of

Atomic Energy, a very powerful entity in Russia. Or built by, or for, the KGB, a completely separate entity, and responsible for all of the intelligence work of Russia. We just don't know the answer.'

The 'suitcase bombs' affair inevitably focused western attention on the issue of nuclear security in Russia. As mentioned earlier, within the Defence Ministry responsibility for security of nuclear weapons lies with the Twelfth Main Directorate, the Twelfth GUMO. Shortly after the end of the Second World War, the Soviet Council of Ministers formed the First Main Directorate with the role of co-ordination of all work on atomic projects. Two years later, a specialist department was created by the Defence Ministry to study US nuclear weapons and their employment. Following the testing of the first Soviet nuclear bomb in 1949, the First Main Directorate and the Defence Ministry department were amalgamated to form a directorate charged with the centralized testing, stockpiling and operation of nuclear weapons.

This new organization was the forerunner of the Twelfth GUMO, which currently maintains large depots in which are kept all tactical and strategic nuclear weapons retrieved from former states of the Soviet Union or withdrawn from service with the Russian armed forces. These are highly secure sites guarded by special Twelfth GUMO units. In addition, the directorate also possesses specially trained troops responsible for transporting nuclear weapons which currently are perceived as being particularly vulnerable to attack from criminal groups or terrorist organizations while in transit.

Although security of nuclear weapons is considered relatively effective, that situation could change. The Twelfth GUMO has also been affected by Russia's severe economic problems which, as mentioned earlier, are severely affecting its armed forces. An indication of this occurred on 5 September 1998, a month after Russia's economic collapse, when five members of a Twelfth GUMO detachment guarding nuclear sites at the port of Novaya Zemlya, Russia's principal nuclear testing facility, killed a senior NCO and, having taken another NCO hostage, attempted to hijack an aircraft. After seizing further hostages, they demanded to be flown to Dagestan in the Caucasus but were subsequently overpowered and disarmed by special forces troops of the Interior Ministry. A month later the head of the Twelfth GUMO, while seeking to allay fears over a breakdown of security at its storage depots, admitted that his troops were not being given any priority over pay and that some were receiving food for the winter instead of their salaries.

Following the incident at Novaya Zemlya, there were two further occurrences of breakdowns of discipline involving military personnel at nuclear facilities: on 11 September a young member of the crew aboard an Akula Class nuclear attack submarine went berserk with a hammer and a submachine gun, killing seven people before locking himself in the vessel's weapons compartment where nuclear, as well as conventional, torpedoes were stored. He was reportedly killed when special forces troops stormed the submarine, although a spokesman for the Northern Fleet later claimed that he had committed suicide. On 20 September, a senior NCO of a detachment of Interior Ministry troops guarding the RT-1 nuclear reprocessing plant at Mayak turned his AK-47 assault rifle on other members of his unit, killing two and wounding another before escaping with his weapon.

The lack of security at civilian facilities, where fissile material is stored, has also given cause for concern. In the words of a CIA report published in September 1998, 'Russian nuclear weapons-usable fissile materials, plutonium and highly enriched uranium, are more vulnerable to theft than nuclear weapons.' According to a more recent report, 'The Next Wave – Urgently Needed New Steps to Control Warheads and Fissile Material' by Matthew Bunn (the Assistant Director of the Science, Technology and Public Policy Program in the Belfer Center for Science and International Affairs at Harvard University's John F. Kennedy School of Government), and published in April 2000 by the Carnegie Endowment for International Peace, the former states of the Soviet Union are estimated to be in possession of approximately 1,350 tons of weapons-usable nuclear material, comprising highly enriched uranium and plutonium, of which 700 tons is contained in nuclear weapons and 650 tons in various other forms. While all the nuclear weapons and 99 per cent of the weapons-usable material are in Russia, quantities significantly large to pose threats are currently stored in civilian nuclear facilities in the Ukraine, Kazakhstan, Belarus, Latvia and Uzbekistan where serious security problems exist. As quoted in Bunn's report, in March 1996, the Director of Central Intelligence, John Deutch, in his testimony before the Permanent Subcommittee on Investigations of the US Senate's Committee on Governmental Affairs, stated that weapons-usable nuclear materials were more accessible than at any previous time due mainly to the collapse of the Soviet Union and the increasingly deteriorating economic problems throughout the region.

During the 1990s there were a number of reported incidents involving the theft of nuclear material from within Russia. During 1992, 1.5 kilograms (over 3 pounds) of weapons-grade highly enriched uranium was stolen from the Luch nuclear research facility at Podolsk, near Moscow, and in July 1993 1.8 kilograms (4 pounds) of 36 per cent enriched uranium were stolen by two sailors from the Andreeva Guna base in the Kola Peninsula, not far from the border with Norway. Subsequently caught and arrested, they stated that they had been ordered by officers to steal the uranium; those investigating the case suspected the possible involvement of an organized crime syndicate.

One highly publicized case involved the theft in 1993 of 4.5 kilograms (10 pounds) of uranium-235 from the Sevmorput naval shipyard, one of the Russian Navy's principal nuclear fuel storage facilities for its Northern Fleet. On 27 November a naval officer, Captain Alexei Tikhomirov, climbed through one of the many holes in the wooden fence surrounding Fuel Storage Area 3-30 and broke the padlock securing the rear door of the building containing nuclear submarine fuel assemblies. The door was connected to an alarm but it had been corroded by the salty sea air and was useless. The three guards supposedly patrolling the area were middle-aged women armed with pistols: not only were they too nervous to use their weapons but were scared of carrying out their rounds at night for fear of being raped. Once inside, Tikhomirov succeeded in breaking off the enriched uranium from three fuel assemblies with the aid of a hacksaw. Minutes later, he left the area in a vehicle driven by an accomplice and headed for the house of his father, a retired captain in the Red Navy and former commander of an SSBN. There he concealed the uranium in the garage.

The theft was discovered on the following morning but only because Tikhomirov had left the padlock lying on the ground in front of the door, to be found by one of the guards doing her rounds. During the following months Tikhomirov's accomplice, a former captain named Oleg Baranov, attempted to find a buyer for the uranium for which he and Tikhomirov were asking 50,000 dollars; among those he reportedly approached was an organized crime group. In June 1994 Tikhomirov's younger brother, Dmitry, a lieutenant on board a nuclear refuelling maintenance vessel who was also involved in the plot as he had briefed his brother on where to find the fuel assemblies, took it upon himself to try and sell the uranium. He asked the help of a fellow officer, who reported the conversation to a senior officer. Shortly afterwards both Captain Alexei Tikhomirov and his brother, along with Oleg Baranov, were arrested and the uranium recovered.

All three men had been driven to such a desperate measure by poverty-induced despair. Alexei Tikhomirov's salary as a captain was equivalent to £140 per month – if he was fortunate enough to receive it. Subsequently tried and found guilty, he was sentenced to between three and five years in prison while Oleg Baranov received three years. Dmitry Tikhomirov received clemency as he had not actually taken part in the theft but was discharged from the Navy.

Following this, up until early 1996 there were five attempted thefts of nuclear submarine highly enriched uranium fuel from Northern Fleet storage depots in the area of Murmansk and Archangel. A Northern Fleet military prosecutor was reported as stating that an organized crime group operating in Murmansk and St Petersburg had made approaches to naval officers, offering between 400,000 and 1 million dollars per kilogram (just over two pounds) of highly enriched uranium. In January 1996, 7 kilograms

(15$\frac{1}{2}$ pounds) of highly enriched uranium were reportedly stolen from the Pacific Fleet base at Sovietskaya Gavan. Subsequently 2.5 kilograms (5$\frac{1}{2}$ pounds) of the material appeared 5,000 miles (8,000 kilometres) away in the hands of a metals trading company in the Baltic city of Kaliningrad.

In November 1993, as recounted by Andrew and Leslie Cockburn in their book *One Point Safe – The Terrifying Threat of Russia's Unwanted Nuclear Arsenal*, an even more serious theft took place at Zlatoust 36, a city in the Urals and one of the centres of Russia's military nuclear complex. Located there was the weapons assembly facility producing MIRV warheads for the ICBMs and SLBMs of the Strategic Rocket Forces and the Navy respectively. Security at the facility, which normally only permitted access to the storage bunkers under strict supervision, had grown lax and on this occasion two men working in the facility succeeded in purloining two warheads and smuggling them out of the plant in the back of a truck. Driving into the city, they headed for a garage where they concealed their highly dangerous booty. It was not until three days later that the warheads were discovered to be missing and the alarm raised. A check of the personnel who had access to the warheads soon pointed the finger of suspicion at the two culprits and shortly afterwards they were arrested and the warheads retrieved. Both were subsequently tried and imprisoned, the entire affair being covered up. The motive for the theft was never revealed although there was speculation that the men might have stolen the warheads for a potential buyer.

In May of the following year, two people were arrested in St Petersburg in possession of 2 kilograms (about 4$\frac{1}{2}$ pounds) of uranium-235 enriched to 98 per cent; while investigations produced no positive evidence, it was suspected that the material had originated from a nuclear plant east of the Urals. In the same month, 10 May, 5.6 grams (less than a quarter of an ounce) of 99 per cent pure plutonium-239 were found in the garage of a retired mechanic, Adolf Jaekle, in the German village Tengen. The discovery was made by chance during a police investigation into Jaekle, who was suspected of involvement in counterfeiting. When questioned, he maintained that he had obtained the plutonium from a Swiss businessman in Basle, known to have commercial connections in Moscow. The businessman denied any involvement in the affair.

It later transpired that the German intelligence service, the Bundesnachtrichtendienst (BND), suspected that the material had been smuggled out of Russia by representatives of a Bulgarian company called Kintex, which was one of four organizations licensed by the Bulgarian government to trade in arms. Kintex was known to have links with Iraq and its dictator Saddam Hussein. During their search of Adolf Jaekle's house, the Federal Criminal Bureau (BKA) reportedly found documentary evidence of contact between him and Iraqi agents. The BND apparently also suspected that Iraqi agents had arranged payment for shipment of the plutonium to Switzerland, believing that funds for such had been deposited in a bank in Zurich. The affair took an even more serious turn when Jaekle claimed that a further 150 grams (6 ounces) of plutonium had possibly already been smuggled out of Russia and cached in Switzerland, information which was passed swiftly to the Swiss authorities. On 8 August six men, a German and five others from the Czech Republic and Slovakia, were also arrested in connection with this affair. Adolf Jaekle was tried in November the following year and sentenced to five and a half years' imprisonment for smuggling weapons-grade plutonium into Germany.

In August 1994, another well-publicized incident took place when German police and officers of Bavaria's State Criminal Bureau (LKA) met Lufthansa Flight 3369 as it landed at Munich airport and arrested a Colombian, Justiniano Torres Benitez, and two other men. At the same time, they seized a case containing a canister holding over 560 grams (1½ pounds) of mixed oxides of plutonium and uranium, of which 408 grams (just over a pound) comprised plutonium dioxide. According to 'Plutonium, Politics and Panic' published by Mark Hibbs in *The Bulletin of the Atomic Scientists*, the major part of the rest of the material comprised uranium dioxide dominated by depleted uranium. Approximately 87 per cent of the plutonium was fissile 239, the remainder was plutonium-240.

The first the Russians knew of the affair was when it appeared in the international press and on television; instead of notifying them, the Germans had leaked the story to the press, declaring that the material was Russian. The story was much hyped by the international media which proceeded to indulge in an orgy of scaremongering, claiming that further amounts of plutonium and highly enriched uranium were being smuggled into Germany where they were being bought by representatives of terrorist groups and countries such as Iraq, Iran and North Korea.

In the event, the entire affair was subsequently revealed to be a 'sting' operation mounted by the BND and the LKA whose agents had approached Torres Benitez in Spain with a request to sell them 4.5 kilograms (10 pounds) of plutonium for 250 million dollars. The latter had agreed to supply one kilogram for 100 million dollars and had subsequently provided a 0.5 gram sample. Thereafter he had travelled to Moscow, returning on 10 August with his two companions and the canister of fissile material. Although the German authorities claimed that the operation had been a success, others disagreed, pointing out that the operation had resulted only in the arrest of three smugglers and that its primary purpose, identification of the source of the plutonium, had not been achieved.

In December 1994, acting on a tip-off from Interpol, police in Prague seized two canisters, containing 2.7 kilograms (6 pounds) of 88.8 per cent enriched uranium-235, from a car parked in a street in the Czech capital. Analysis found the material to comprise almost 88 per cent uranium-235 and 11 per cent uranium-238 with traces of uranium-234 and 236, minor isotopes not found in fresh fuel, suggesting that the material had been irradiated in a reactor and then reprocessed in a plutonium separation plant.

By late January 1995 three men, a Ukrainian, a Belarussian and a Czech, had been arrested in connection with this affair. It transpired that the uranium had been stolen and smuggled out of Russia in to Prague where it had been awaiting a buyer when it was seized. The Czech authorities were unable to determine its source despite attempts made to identify its 'fingerprint', the unique signature left on fissile material by the process of enriching or burning. No two nuclear processing facilities are identical and thus leave their individual signatures on every batch of uranium, in theory enabling its source to be identified. As the material was in the form of uranium dioxide, some experts in the West suspected that it had been stolen from a plant producing naval reactor fuel. A large number of Soviet submarines were powered by uranium dioxide fuel which allowed the high burn-up required for lengthy operations without the requirement for refuelling. While the majority of Soviet submarine fuel was enriched to 30 per cent and 60 per cent, being produced at Vladivostok, Serodvinsk and Severomorsk, a certain amount was enriched to over 80 per cent.

In March 1997, a group of criminals were arrested in the town of Rubtsovsk, south of Novosibirsk in western Siberia near the border with Kazakhstan, in possession of a quantity of uranium-235. More members of the group were apprehended at Berdsk, another town in the same area where they were planning to hand over the uranium to prospective buyers who were in fact undercover agents of the Novosibirsk County police. Yet again, during investigations into the theft, efforts to trace the source of the uranium proved unsuccessful. Later in the year, a Russian team visiting the abandoned Sukhimi research centre in the Abkhazia region of Georgia discovered that 2 kilograms (4.4 pounds) of 90 per cent highly enriched uranium had disappeared from the facility which had been abandoned in 1993 during the Abkhaz civil war. At the time of writing, they are still missing. In September, Russian police seized 3.8 kilograms (8.4 pounds) of stolen uranium-238 and 2 kilograms (4.4 pounds) of red mercury oxide concealed in a house in Ivanov, a town in the north Caucasus. At the same time, several members of a gang were arrested; they had been attempting to sell the material to prospective buyers in Moscow, the Baltic States and elsewhere. It had been stolen from the nuclear research centre at Sarov, formerly known as Arzamas-16, from where a container of fissile material had previously disappeared in 1994.

In the latter part of 1998, a group of workers at one of the Minatom facilities in the Chelyabinsk region, which included the nuclear weapons design laboratory at Snezhinsk, the processing plant at Ozersk and the nuclear weapons assembly and dismantling facility at Trekhgorny, attempted to steal 18.5 kilograms (40 pounds) of radioactive material later described by Russian officials as being suitable for use in the assembly of a nuclear weapon.

In November of that year, an employee at a leading Russian nuclear weapons design institute was arrested for spying for Iraq. It was precisely to prevent such occurrences that the CTR Program has also channelled resources into defence conversion programmes which includes employment by the International Scientific and Technical Corporation, an organization formed under CTR auspices, of some 24,000 scientists previously involved in the Soviet defence establishment. The purpose of this was to prevent scientists being tempted by offers from regimes such as those of Iran, Iraq and North Korea who were keen to acquire their expertise for their own nuclear weapon development programmes.

During the last decade, a considerable amount of evidence came to light that certain countries were seeking to develop a military nuclear capability, notably Iraq, Iran, Libya and North Korea. During the Gulf War in 1991, Iraq succeeded in concealing much of its programme of weapons of mass destruction from Coalition bombers and cruise missiles: the nuclear complexes at Tarmiya and Ash Sharqat were damaged but not destroyed while the most important facility, at Al Atheer, remained intact. Information from an Iraqi defector, a leading nuclear physicist, and satellite photographic surveillance subsequently revealed the presence of calutrons (electro-magnetic systems for enriching uranium) which were buried by the Iraqis pending visits by UN inspection teams and retrieved thereafter. These were later destroyed but by 1995 it was evident that the Iraqis had changed tack and were seeking weapons-grade uranium and plutonium, thus dispensing with the need for enrichment facilities.

Iraq used its covert procurement networks to source material and equipment, despatching agents throughout the former Soviet Union. In 1995 it was successful in obtaining 120 missile guidance gyroscope systems removed from Russian Navy SLBMs. Three years later, the CIA warned that Iraq was seeking to purchase either fissile material or complete nuclear weapons.

Iran has also been active in searching for nuclear weapons and technology in the former Soviet states. In 1992 Iranian agents were spotted visiting nuclear facilities, in particular in Kazakhstan where they appeared at Ust-Kamenogorsk, Semipalatinsk and Aktau with a list of items they required for the Iranian nuclear weapons programme. Kazakhstan was by then, however, unwilling to upset the United States and the West with whom it was fast establishing close links and thus turned down their approaches. Nothing daunted, Iran turned to the Russians, dangling as bait a multi-million-dollar contract to complete the construction of a nuclear power station, containing two 1,000-megawatt light-water reactors, at Bushehr situated 750 kilometres (466 miles) south of Teheran on the coast of the Persian Gulf.

During 1994 Viktor Mikhailov, the Minister of Nuclear Energy and head of Minatom, carried out a number of visits to Iran. On 8 January 1995 he signed a contract for the Bushehr project with Iran's Atomic Energy Organization, which was headed by Reza Amrollahi, the Iranian Vice-President who was also responsible for his country's nuclear weapon development programme. According to Andrew and Leslie Cockburn in their book *One Point Safe*, the contract was for the construction of 'Block No. 1' at the nuclear power facility at Bushehr. Two months later, however, a copy of a protocol relating to the contract was passed to a member of the US Embassy in Moscow, revealing that among the facilities to be supplied by the Russians were a gas centrifuge and a desalination plant. This caused alarm in Washington, as a gas centrifuge is a system used for enrichment of uranium while a nuclear-powered desalination plant of the type supplied by the Russians produced, as a by-product, plutonium of a very high level of purity.

Approaches to the Russians, and Mikhailov in particular, to try and persuade them not to proceed with the deal proved fruitless. When the news of the sale of the two reactors was made public, however, there was a storm of protest led by Professor Alexei Yablokov who, despite Mikhailov's statements to the contrary, knew that plutonium could be extracted from spent fuel from such plants. Yablokov investigated the details of the sale and discovered the protocol, which resulted in his publishing an article in *Izvestia*, giving full details. This gave the Americans the opportunity to publicize the issue which had hitherto been kept tightly under wraps. In May President Bill Clinton, equipped with a comprehensive report on the entire Iranian military nuclear development programme, attended a summit in Moscow during which he discussed the matter with President Boris Yeltsin. The latter refused to halt the sale of the two reactors but agreed to block that of the gas centrifuge which, he agreed, could be used in the production of nuclear weapons.

In August 1995, however, following the visit of an Iranian delegation led by Reza Amrollahi, the Russians signed a second contract with Iran for the supply of two 400-megawatt reactors for the Neka nuclear research complex in northern Iran which is believed by western experts to be part of the Iranian military nuclear research programme. In September, it was reported that China was constructing a calutron at the nuclear research establishment at Karaj, some 160 kilometres (100 miles) north-west of Teheran. The same report disclosed that large numbers of Russian scientists were working at Iran's eleven nuclear research establishments, of which only five were open to international scrutiny.

While the idea of Iraq and Iran possessing a military nuclear capability is one nightmare scenario for the West, that of terrorists laying their hands on them is another. There have been numerous reports that Al Qaida, the Islamic fundamentalist organization headed by Osama bin Laden, has long been seeking to acquire nuclear weapons through its contacts in the Ukraine and other former states of the Soviet Union. Indeed, as mentioned in Matthew Bunn's report 'The Next Wave', the United States has issued a federal indictment of bin Laden and his organization, charging that he and others have on various occasions attempted to acquire components for nuclear weapons.

Another group known to have sought nuclear material and technology is the Japanese cult Aum Shinrikyo, which was responsible in March 1995 for the sarin nerve agent attack on the Tokyo subway. The group had recruited large numbers of members in Russia, among them scientists from Moscow State University and members of staff of the Kurchatov Research Institute in Moscow which possessed relatively large quantities of weapons-usable highly enriched uranium. It is known that a senior member of the cult, Kiyohide Hayakawa, carried out many visits to Russia to procure weapons and other equipment.

Such was the growing concern over the poor physical security and careless accounting at nuclear sites in Russia that the United States instituted a series of programmes to improve the security of, and accounting procedures for, nuclear weapons and fissile material in the former Soviet Union. These included a material protection, control and accounting (MPC&A) Program, funded by the US Department of Energy and designed to improve security and accounting of all nuclear materials at sites throughout former Soviet states; the construction at Mayak of a special secure storage facility, funded by the Department of Defense, for fissile material extracted from dismantled weapons and spent fuel assemblies; provision of equipment for upgrading of security of nuclear weapon storage facilities and transport; and programmes for the removal of weapons-usable nuclear material from sites considered to be vulnerable. In addition, the Department of Defense and other US agencies such as the Department of Energy, Federal Bureau of Investigation and the US Customs Service are assisting former Soviet states in improving the capabilities of their own law enforcement agencies to combat the smuggling of nuclear materials.

Meanwhile, the thefts of fissile and radioactive material have continued in various parts of the former Soviet Union. In September 1999, six people were arrested in Vladivostok while trying to sell 6 kilograms (13 pounds) of uranium-238 to undercover police officers posing as prospective buyers; the material was subsequently reported as having been stolen from a shipyard in the far east where

Russian Navy nuclear submarines were serviced. During the following month, two people were arrested by police in western Ukraine after being caught smuggling 24 kilograms (53 pounds) of uranium from Krasnoyarsk County in Russia. During February 2000 three men were arrested in Alma Ata, the capital of Kazakhstan, after being found in possession of 530 grams of uranium (nearly $1^1/_2$ pounds); in the city of Ussuriysk two military officers were apprehended while attempting to sell 20 grams (about an ounce) of radioactive strontium. The end of February saw police arrest a group of five men in Donetsk, eastern Ukraine, who were trying to sell twenty-eight containers of radioactive strontium-90. At the beginning of April, customs officials in Uzbekistan stopped a truck near the border with Kazakhstan and seized ten steel containers of unidentified radioactive material; the vehicle and driver were Iranian but the latter maintained that his destination was not Iran, but Pakistan.

Despite the efforts of the United States and other countries to reduce the dangers from Russia's nuclear stockpile, its size and infrastructure are such that there is still a very long way to go before its hazards are removed completely. Meanwhile, deteriorating safeguards still pose the threat of an unauthorized missile launch, while poor standards of security and lax accounting in many civilian nuclear establishments are such that nuclear material is still vulnerable to theft. While such conditions exist, the threat of a nuclear holocaust is still present.

AFTER DESERT STORM

igh technology and new weapon systems played principal roles during the Gulf War, enabling Coalition forces to overcome those of the Iraqi dictator Saddam Hussein within forty-four days.

At 4.45 p.m. local time on 16 January 1991, at a US Airforce (USAF) base at Khamis Mushayt in Saudi Arabia, pilots and ground crew of the 37th Tactical Fighter Wing were preparing their forty-two F-117A Stealth aircraft for a raid in the early hours of the following day on the heavily defended capital, Baghdad. Possessing no guns or radar, the F-117A relied solely on technology to protect it during its mission. Coated in radar-absorbent material, the aircraft's skin would soak up much of any energy aimed at it, its unconventional shape deflecting any further beams away from the interrogating transmitter. Indeed, the radar signature of the F-117A is the same as a small bird or large insect.

Its existence officially denied until six years after it entered service in 1982, the F-117A is a single-seat high-subsonic aircraft powered by two General Electric F404 engines located above the fuselage within deep recesses to minimize their infra-red signature. Costing 45 million dollars, it is equipped with sophisticated navigation and attack systems integrated into a state-of-the-art digital avionics suite designed to increase its mission effectiveness and reduce pilot workload, with detailed planning for missions into high-risk target areas being carried out by an automated mission planning system.

Its primary role being low-level precision strike, the F-117A is armed with air-to-ground missiles and laser-guided bombs carried in two internal weapon bays. Weapons carried by F-117As during the Gulf War included the GBU-27 improved 2,000-pound bomb and the Mk.82 500-pound bomb, both fitted with the Paveway III laser guidance system. The aircraft is equipped with a forward-looking infra-red (FLIR) system producing high-definition images on a monitor in the instrument panel, enabling the pilot to view and identify a target. He then switches to a second downward-looking infra-red system, boresighted with a laser target designator, locks the laser on to a target and at an appropriate point releases his laser-guided bombs which, as will be explained later in this chapter, home in on the infra-red energy reflected from the target.

At 2.35 a.m. local time on 17 January, 966 kilometres (600 miles) away in the Persian Gulf, another high-technology weapon was about to be launched against Saddam Hussein, this time an unmanned RGM-109 Tomahawk cruise missile. Ten minutes later on board the cruiser USS *Bunker Hill* and other warships, night turned to day with flame erupting from the vessels' decks as Tomahawks burst out of their launchers, hurtling up into the air before deploying their small, stubby wings and heading away into the night towards Baghdad. Meanwhile, UGM-109 Tomahawks burst forth from the sea, having been launched from submarines below the surface. Just over fifty minutes later, the night was filled with explosions and balls of flame as the missiles impacted on their targets, the sky illuminated by glowing balls of tracer and the muzzle flashes of anti-aircraft weapons as Iraqi gunners fired wildly into the air, desperately attempting to bring down the invisible enemy. Such was the intensity of the anti-aircraft fire that eyewitnesses later described it as an 'awesome fireworks display'.

To the F-117A pilots flying through the storm of anti-aircraft fire on that first night of the war, it seemed inevitable that they would be hit – but in the event all survived unscathed, having successfully completed strikes against command posts and communications centres as well as radar and surface-to-air missile sites. Air Vice Marshal Bill Wratten of the Royal Air Force, deputy commander of British forces during the Gulf War, later commented, 'I think everybody was well pleased with the success of the Stealth fighter, the F-117. It did all that was expected and hoped of it. It went in, as far as we know, unseen and came out unseen. The very early waves were targeted against the Iraqi communications systems for obvious reasons. Now the fact that he [Saddam Hussein] stopped broadcasting at the precise time on target of the first wave was reasonable indication of that first wave being successful.'

As Colonel John Warden of the USAF's War Fighting Unit later pointed out, 'Within the first ten minutes of the war, there had been attacks on the telephone system, the electrical system, on all of the sector operations centres, the national air defence operations centres, the associated intercept operations centres, and on significant command posts at strategic and operational levels. This happened across the entire breadth of the country and it happened, for practical purposes, simultaneously. Once we had made the first attack, he [Saddam Hussein] was doomed because we had imposed strategic paralysis from which he did not recover.'

Colonel Warden's observations on that first night's attacks on Baghdad were all too accurate. By the end of that first night of air strikes, the Iraqis realized they were deaf, dumb and blind. Stealth technology had not only received its baptism of fire but had also dramatically proved its worth in more than one way. In addition to knocking out the entire Iraqi command and communications system in Baghdad, the Stealth aircraft had also proved that they were capable of achieving the same results as large numbers of conventional aircraft requiring considerable support.

As Lieutenant Colonel David Deptula, a USAF war planner, explained: 'What Stealth allows you to do is to obviate the need for large force packaging that you need with conventional aircraft assets. You don't need all the suppression of enemy air defences aircraft, what we call SEAD, to go along with Stealth to protect them. That allows you to free up a whole series of assets to strike a wide array of targets simultaneously. An example of this took place early on in the war when we had a conventional attack package consisting of four Saudi Tornadoes, and four A-6s. Since it was relatively early on in the conflict, these were escorted by four F-4Gs designed to suppress enemy air defences, five EA-6Bs, electronic combat jamming aircraft, and twenty-one F/A-18 Hornets carrying high-speed anti-radiation missiles to take out surface-to-air missile sites. A total of thirty-eight aircraft to get four bomb droppers across one target. At the same time, we had twenty-one F-117s attacking thirty-eight targets. That is the value of Stealth – it allows you to accomplish much more than if you only had conventional aircraft.'

Dawn on 17 January revealed to the Iraqis the appalling scale of destruction and havoc wreaked by the F-117As and cruise missiles during that first night. Thereafter the barrage continued remorselessly. In the Persian Gulf, more of the 1.3 million-dollar missiles lanced upwards from launchers on the battleships USS *Missouri* and *Wisconsin* and headed for Baghdad. Guided by its terrain-following radar, each missile followed its individually pre-programmed route as it flew towards its own target.

The Tomahawk is a 6-metre (20-foot) long missile powered in the initial stage of its flight by a rocket that launches it from its tube on board a ship or submarine. Thereafter, a small turbofan cuts in and the missile proceeds to fly at a speed of approximately 885 kilometres per hour (550 miles per hour) on a course towards its target, initially steered by an inertial guidance system that uses gyroscopes and sensors to govern changes of course and speed. Once it reaches a coastline, another more precise system, called TERCOM, takes over and navigates by scanning the surrounding landscape at pre-set intervals, measuring altitude readings and comparing them to pre-stored data in the computer's memory. Flying at altitudes between 30 and 90 metres (100 to 300 feet), the missile follows the contours of the terrain. As it nears its target, another guidance system takes control. Called the Digital Scene Matching Area Correlator (DSMAC), it digitally photographs the target area and compares the image to one already stored in its memory, resulting in final adjustments being made to the Tomahawk's course as it begins its approach to the target.

Such were the heavy defences in and around Baghdad that only cruise missiles were employed in attacks on the city during daylight. Aircraft were, however, used during the day on targets elsewhere, principally against Iraqi positions in Kuwait and near the Saudi border. As dusk fell on 17 January and the aircraft returned from their first day of operations, preparations were being made for a second night of attacks. Among the aircraft employed on nocturnal raids was the venerable F-111, an aircraft that had been in service with the USAF for twenty-five years. Although elderly, it carried an array of sophisticated bombs, precision-guided munitions popularly known as 'smart bombs'. Costing 80,000 dollars apiece, these are conventional bombs fitted with a laser-seeking sensor, a simple guidance mechanism and steering fins on the nose. They are, however, over four times more accurate than their conventional counterparts.

A 'dumb' bomb, as conventional weapons are now called, will fall along a parabolic trajectory governed by a combination of forces: gravity, wind resistance and the forward velocity of the launching aircraft. However, dumb bombs are also affected by other factors, principally winds, air currents, aerodynamics and structural asymmetrics, which cause them to deviate from their intended path. Such factors would result in half of a stick of four dumb bombs dropped from an altitude of about 3,000 metres (10,000 feet) missing the aiming point on the ground by up to one-eighth of a mile, an area of lethality known as the circular error probability (CEP). During the Second World War, bombs dropped from high altitudes on Germany in daylight raids by USAF B-17 Flying Fortresses landed as much as a mile from their targets, resulting in a CEP of 1,015 metres (3,300 feet). This meant that 9,000 bombs would be needed to hit a small target area measuring 18.5 metres (60 feet) by nearly 31 metres (100 feet). Almost 1,000 B-17s would have been required to drop such a massive amount of ordnance, a number beyond the capabilities of any contemporary air force in terms of both aircraft and aircrew.

It was during the Vietnam War that tests were conducted with laser-guided bombs. Since then, advances in technology have resulted in munitions of increasing precision and such is the accuracy of current weapon systems that a bomb can be guided precisely to the required point of impact. Such a high level of accuracy, producing devastating results with the minimum of collateral damage, is achieved by the attacking aircraft illuminating a target with the invisible beam of a laser emitting coded pulses of infra-red light. In effect, the target acts as a laser lighthouse, reflecting the infra-red energy back into the sky in the form of a cone. When first developed, the system was classified as top secret and codenamed Pave Tac.

A typical attack carried out by two F-111s would see the Pave Tac aircraft arriving at the target area with the weapons officer's radar and the Pave Tac infra-red detector set observing it. The laser provides information about the target, providing information on range to it, which allows the pilot to position his aircraft to provide the best opportunity for the sensor on the other aircraft to 'see' the target. The weapons officer switches to a video view of the target as seen by the Pave Tac system and maintains the laser's lock on the target. Meanwhile, the bomb from the second aircraft has been released and is flying down into the centre of the cone of infra-red light, at the point of which is the target. The system is so precise that it allows destruction of the target with minimal collateral damage and loss of life within the immediate surrounding area.

On the night of 17 January, the second wave of air strikes on Iraq took place but in the early hours of the following day Iraq struck back, launching eight ballistic missiles against Israel.

Until then, the Coalition forces in Saudi Arabia had not taken seriously the threat of Iraq using its missiles which were based on a modified version of the Scud-B short range ballistic missile (SRBM). Developed in the 1960s by the Russians, the Scud had the capability to deliver conventional high-explosive, chemical or nuclear warheads. Not a particularly accurate weapon, it was intended for use against large targets such as major storage dumps, marshalling areas and airfields. The initial version, designated by NATO as the SS-1B Scud-A, was mounted on a tracked chassis, being raised into the vertical position from a small platform. A larger version, the SS-1C Scud-B, was subsequently produced. With a maximum range of 280 kilometres (174 miles), it was carried in a protective casing on a large MAZ-543 eight-wheeled transporter that also accommodated all the necessary support elements for the missile.

Iraq's involvement with ballistic missiles had begun during the previous decade when, while at war with Iran, it had invested heavily in missile research and development, using technology, equipment and components acquired from the West. The main missile development centre was Saad 16, located outside Mosul in northern Iraq, which was constructed in strict secrecy by a consortium of European countries, notably Austria and West Germany. A web of Swiss, West German and Austrian companies provided high technology equipment and systems covertly sourced from Britain, Europe and the United States.

In 1984 Iraq joined forces with Egypt and Argentina to develop a missile. Designated Condor-2, it was a two-stage solid-fuel-powered missile with a payload capacity of 500 kilograms (1,100 pounds) and a maximum range of 1,000 kilometres (620 miles). Meanwhile, Iraq purchased a number of Scud-Bs from the Soviet Union and proceeded to modify them by reducing the 1,000-kilogram (2,200-pound) warhead to 500 kilograms (1,100 pounds) and enlarging the size of the fuel tanks in order to increase the maximum range to 600 kilometres (373 miles). The modified missile, redesignated 'Al-Hussein', was subsequently used with devastating effect against Iranian cities in the final stages of the Iran–Iraq War of 1980–8.

During 1987 Iraq additionally acquired over 120 Badr-2000 missiles from Egypt, also using them to blitz Iran. These were modified Scud-Bs too, having a reduced payload of 275 kilograms (605 pounds) and a range of 600 kilometres (373 miles). Meanwhile, Egypt shipped three prototype Condor-2 missiles to Iraq for trial use against Iran and in the following year supplied sixteen more. It was estimated that Iraq used approximately 360 missiles during the war with Iran, launching some 200 over a period of forty days between February and April 1988.

In December 1989 the Iraqis tested an intermediate range ballistic missile (IRBM), claiming it had a range of 2,000 kilometres (1,243 miles). Designated Al Aabed, it comprised a three-stage type powered by five Scud boosters and carried a 750-kilogram (1,650-pound) warhead. In November 1990 they claimed to have tested another, designated Al Hijara, also with a range of 2,000 kilometres. The appearance of these two missiles caused concern as it meant that the Iraqis possessed the capability to reach Israel, Saudi Arabia and the Gulf States.

The eight Scuds that landed in the area of Tel Aviv on 18 January fortunately caused only limited damage, although sixty-eight people were injured. However, the inaccuracy of the missile was irrelevant in such circumstances; with a target as large as a city the size of Tel Aviv, a Scud would cause damage wherever it fell. The lack of physical damage also mattered little as the political impact of the attack was considerable and sent ripples reverberating around the world. Indeed, this had been the precise objective behind the use of such an imprecise weapon. While on this occasion the missiles had been armed with conventional high explosive, it was all too obvious that in further attacks against Israel or Coalition forces the Iraqis might use chemical warheads. It was well known that they had used chemical weapons during the Iran–Iraq War; on 16 March 1988 they had done so against the Kurdish town of Halabja, massacring its occupants.

It was clear that the Iraqi missiles, whether or not they were carrying chemical warheads, had to be stopped and the main hope of doing so lay in the US Army's MIM-104 Patriot Tactical Air Defence Missile System, units of which were rushed by air to the Gulf to join the Coalition forces, some being deployed to Israel.

Developed as an anti-aircraft weapon during the late 1970s, the Patriot was modified in the mid-1980s to provide defence against ballistic missiles also. The 5.38-metre (17.5-foot) long missile is a single-stage solid-fuel rocket-motor powered type giving a speed of Mach 3. Weighing 1,000 kilograms (2,200 pounds) and carrying a 100-kilogram (221-pound) high-explosive fragmentation warhead, it has an effective range of between 65 and 68 kilometres (40 to 42 miles) and an altitude ceiling of 24,000 metres (78,740 feet).

Each Patriot unit is equipped with eight launchers, which also serve as containers for transportation and storage, each launcher having four missiles. The system is mobile, each four-missile launcher is mounted on a wheeled trailer. The system's fire control unit comprises the MPQ-53 phased array radar which performs IFF (Identification Friend or Foe) interrogation, target acquisition, tracking and missile guidance; the MSQ-104 engagement control station which accommodates the system's fire and operational status control computer; and the MJQ-24 power plant.

Once a target has been detected, the Patriot is launched and is initially steered to the target by the missile's guidance system, which turns it towards the target as it flies into the radar's beam. Thereafter the system's computer directs the missile to the target until it becomes semi-active as its own radar receiver steers it to the point of interception.

During the following weeks of the Gulf War, much publicity was given to the Patriot which was perceived, along with the F-117A Stealth fighter, cruise missiles and laser-guided bombs, as yet another example of the West's technical supremacy. The incoming Al-Hussein missiles were mostly detected at a range of some 112 kilometres (70 miles) and were engaged at 16 and 32 kilometres (10 and 20 miles). Television audiences were able to watch and marvel as Patriots soared upwards into the night skies over Israel and Saudi Arabia, intercepting the Iraqi missiles with thunderous explosions and impressive balls of flame. In fact, those attempting to shoot down the Iraqi missiles faced an extremely difficult problem.

At the point of launching, an Al-Hussein missile weighed just over 5 tons, most of which comprised liquid propellant. At the top of its trajectory it would reach an altitude of over 150 kilometres (93 miles) before heading down towards its target; at this point it would be detected by a Patriot battery's radar whose high-speed computers would immediately calculate its trajectory velocity and potential impact point. With the missile within range at under 68.5 kilometres (42.5 miles), a Patriot would be launched and in theory would intercept the Al-Hussein and destroy it. However, in this instance the theory was wrong.

The original Scud-B was a large slow missile, providing an easy target. The Al-Hussein, however, not only had increased range but also greater speed, travelling at approximately 8,000 kilometres (5,000 miles) per hour, and thus intercepting it was far more difficult. A further problem was that if the missiles re-entered the Earth's atmosphere at an angle, which they appear to have done on a number of occasions, unequal aerodynamic forces caused their bodies to break up. The large pieces of debris falling to earth created solid tracks on the Patriot radars, which assumed they were missiles; on the first night that they were used in Tel Aviv, twenty-eight Patriots, costing 17 million dollars, were launched at the debris of five Al-Hussein missiles.

Once it was realized that the missiles were breaking up, the Patriot radar operators quickly learned to distinguish between debris and the warheads and to engage the latter. As was later pointed out, however, the missile debris falling earthwards at a speed of some 800 kilometres per hour (500 miles per hour) could still kill or certainly cause considerable damage.

Saddam Hussein's objective in launching his missiles against Israel was, however, political rather than military. He was attempting to draw Israel into the war, putting pressure on the Arab elements within the Coalition. His hope was that they would withdraw from it rather than fight on the same side as Israel against an Arab nation. Patriot was deployed to Israel to prevent just such a situation arising and thus, from a political point of view, proved a success.

While the Iraqis' fixed-missile launch sites were attacked and destroyed by air strikes during an early stage of the war, the mobile launchers continued to cause a problem. British and US special forces were given the task of hunting them down but they were difficult to locate, the Iraqis having dispersed them widely, concealing them from airborne and satellite surveillance under bridges and highway flyovers. Emerging to launch their missiles, the transporter/launchers would return to hiding where they would rendezvous with support vehicles and reload. A subsequent study by the Chief of Staff of the USAF, General Merrill McPeak, estimated that between 18 January and 26 February 1991 the Iraqis launched forty missiles against Israel and forty-six against Saudi Arabia.

Location and destruction of the mobile launch vehicles became a top priority for the Coalition in its efforts to prevent Saddam Hussein achieving his aim of drawing Israel into the war. The answer to the problem of locating them was found in the airborne element of JSTARS, the acronym for the US Army/USAF Joint Surveillance Target Attack Radar System, which at that time was still under development.

Designed to carry out airborne surveillance from a stand-off distance of 250 kilometres (155 miles), JSTARS is capable of detecting, locating and tracking fixed and mobile targets on the ground over an area of more than 20,000 square kilometres (7,720 square miles) in all weather conditions, providing commanders with near real-time data. Installed in modified Boeing 707-300Bs designated E-8C STARS, the system's main element is the

Northrop/Grumman AN/APY-3 high performance, multi-mode airborne radar that detects, locates and classifies ground targets. The system is interface with the US Army's Ground Station Module (GSM) via a special data link, the Surveillance Control Data Link (SCDL), to transmit and receive target data. With a ceiling of 12,500 metres (41,000 feet), the E-8C aircraft's operating altitude is 10,700 metres (35,000 feet). Its maximum range is 4,480 kilometres (2,800 miles) and it has an operational endurance of eleven hours without refuelling. The number of crew varies between twenty-one and thirty-four.

On board the E-8C aircraft, radar operators are positioned at consoles that incorporate displays on which are electronically generated maps of sectors of the areas under surveillance, showing roads, rivers, forests and other topographical features. Overlaid on to these are displays of yellow dots, each of which represents a moving object. These are assembled over a period of some twenty to thirty minutes to provide a pattern from which the operator can try to assess what is happening in his sector of responsibility. If he detects organized movement or something that is indicative of, for example, a column of moving vehicles, a synthetic aperture radar picture will be taken of that sector to identify the items detected. Such methods proved highly successful in that they resulted in the detection and location of Iraqi assembly areas and, through the use of imagery analysers, the types of vehicles in them.

Initially JSTARS was used to concentrate on Iraqi armoured formations but once the Iraqis commenced their ballistic missile attacks, it was thereafter used to assist in locating the mobile launchers. On several occasions, the system located launch sites and was able to direct aircraft to them, resulting in several cases in interdiction before launches occurred.

JSTARS' downlink capabilities proved especially valuable, enabling surveillance imagery seen in the aircraft to be transmitted simultaneously to ground units. Early in the war, in January 1991, elements of three Iraqi divisions crossed the border in three columns from Kuwait into Saudi Arabia. The easternmost column, comprising over forty tanks and a number of armoured personnel carriers of the 5th Mechanized Division, advanced on the coastal resort and oil town of Khafji 12 kilometres (8 miles) south of the border. It was deserted at the time, its 15,000 inhabitants having been having been evacuated as the town was within range of Iraqi artillery located in the south of Kuwait.

At 8 p.m. on the night of 29 January, the Iraqis encountered Saudi and Qatari troops together with a screening force of US marines of the 1st Marine Division. By 9.30 p.m. air support had arrived, including an E-8C JSTARS which during the following four days of fighting proved invaluable in defeating the Iraqi attack, detecting and tracking the movements of the Iraqi forces and passing information to commanders on the ground while also directing 100 sorties by F-15 aircraft, and forty by F-16s, against ground targets. At one point, it observed a column of enemy armour heading from the border town of Wafra towards Khafji, and directed further air attacks against it; the Iraqi armour never reached the town. During the latter part of the battle, B-52 bombers were diverted for strikes against JSTARS-designated targets.

While JSTARS provided such invaluable support to ground forces, the E-3 Sentry AWACS (Airborne Warning And Control System) did likewise for Coalition aircraft, providing all-weather surveillance, command, control and communications support.

The E-3 Sentry is a modified Boeing 707-320, easily recognized by its rotating 9-metre (30-foot) diameter radar dome mounted above the fuselage. With a ceiling of over 8,840 metres (29,000 feet) and endurance of over eight hours before refuelling, it is equipped with a radar subsystem capable of surveillance over land and water from the Earth's surface right up to the stratosphere. It will detect low-flying aircraft at ranges of over 320 kilometres (200 miles) and medium and high altitude targets at greater distances. Working in combination with an Identification Friend or Foe (IFF) subsystem, the radar can identify and track friendly or hostile aircraft by eliminating ground clutter. Other subsystems comprise communications, navigation and computers for data processing. Radar operators, stationed at consoles which show data in graphic and tabular format, carry out functions including surveillance, identification, weapons control, battle management and communications.

The radar and computer subsystems are capable of acquiring and displaying broad and detailed battlefield data as events occur, including position, tracking and status information relating to aircraft and vessels, both friendly and hostile, which can be transmitted to major command and control centres on land or at sea. When acting in support of air-to-ground operations, the E-3 Sentry AWACS can supply information required for reconnaissance, interdiction and close air support for ground forces, while also supplying commanders of air operations with information essential for control of the air battle. Furthermore, as part of an air defence system, it can detect, identify and track hostile aircraft, directing fighters to intercept them.

During the Gulf War, E-3 Sentry AWACS aircraft were among the first to deploy to Saudi Arabia, thereafter establishing twenty-four-hour radar surveillance on Iraq. Flying over 400 missions in over 5,000 hours on-station, they provided surveillance and control for more than 120,000 sorties flown by Coalition aircraft while also providing up-to-the-minute information on enemy deployments for senior commanders.

By the third week of Operation Desert Storm, the Coalition had air superiority and thus virtual freedom of the skies. This resulted in the decision to intensify bombing raids over Iraq and in so doing to call on another piece of technology which, like JSTARS, was still under development: the Thermal Imaging Airborne Laser Designator (TIALD). Fitted to the Tornado GR1 aircraft of the Royal Air Force, TIALD represented the very latest in 'smart' electro-optical precision guidance systems.

Contained in a pod fastened to the belly of an aircraft's fuselage, TIALD comprises an infra-red thermal imager (TI), a television (TV) sensor, a laser rangefinder/designator, stabilized optics and an automatic video tracking system. A steerable sensor head permits the common sightline of the TI, TV sensor and laser rangefinder/designator to be directed on to targets by either the operator or the aircraft's avionics systems. The TI has the capability to penetrate smoke and haze, the infra-red telescope providing a wide field-of-view, which is used initially for target acquisition, and a narrow one for recognition of the target and aiming of the laser beam. A further 2× and 4× magnification can be achieved through use of an electronic zoom. The TV sensor is equipped with a narrow field-of-view lens and is used to provide images when conditions are such that the contrast in the TI image is adversely affected or when countermeasures are being employed.

The role of TIALD is to steer air-dropped laser-guided munitions directly to their targets. Prior to a mission, target co-ordinates are entered into the aircraft's main computer and en route to the target the operator will boresight the radar to that position. At a distance of some 32 kilometres (20 miles) from the target, using the system's slave mode, he will direct TIALD to observe in the same direction as the radar; and at a range of 24 kilometres (15 miles) will select the narrow field-of-view to magnify the target. Having recognized it, he will use a manual control device to place an aiming graticule precisely over the target, thereafter engaging the video tracking system which will automatically maintain the beam from the laser designator on the target. In normal circumstances the beam will stay switched on for thirty seconds until bomb impact, remaining on the first target for only a few seconds before being switched to a second target to direct bombs which have been released and are already dropping towards it.

On 19 December 1990, only a month before the beginning of hostilities in the Gulf, the British Ministry of Defence decided to accelerate production of TIALD. The programme was given top priority and less than two months later the system entered service with the RAF wing based at Tabuk, in Saudi Arabia. In early February 1991 five modified Tornado GR1s, two TIALD pods and ten crews were deployed to guide in the bombs of fourteen other Tornado GR1s. Three days after they arrived in the Gulf, the first TIALD-led sorties were carried out against fourteen airfields and thereafter continued throughout the rest of the conflict. Targets included five strategically important bridges and fourteen airfields throughout Iraq, with individual targets comprising hardened aircraft shelters, runways, fuel storage areas, ammunition and bomb dumps and aircrew facilities. A total of 229 direct hits by TIALD-directed laser-guided bombs was recorded.

The true value of laser-guided munitions in the Gulf War is illustrated by the fact that of the 88,500 tons of bombs dropped by Coalition air forces during the conflict, only 8 per cent (7,080 tons) were precision-guided. That percentage, however, destroyed over 50 per cent of targets.

By the middle of February the Iraqi air force had been systematically destroyed, or had fled for sanctuary to Iran, and Coalition commanders were thus able to turn their attention to the impending ground war. Bombardment of Iraqi formations now became the responsibility of long-range artillery and in particular another newly developed system, the Multi-Rocket Launch Rocket System (MLRS).

The MLRS is a rocket artillery system mounted on a high mobility stretched M2 Bradley chassis and crewed by three men: commander, driver and gunner. The M270 launcher, containing twelve rockets loaded in two six-round pods, is an automated self-loading unit equipped with a self-aiming system and a fire control computer. Rockets can either be fired individually or in ripples of two to twelve in less than sixty seconds, the fire control computer ensuring that accuracy is maintained by re-aiming the launcher between rounds.

MLRS fires a number of different projectiles. The standard MLRS surface-to-surface rocket contains 644 M77 anti-personnel bomblet munitions, which are dispensed in mid-air and are armed in mid-air as they fall to earth, a drag-ribbon system ensuring that they land correctly. One MLRS salvo from a launcher can dispense up to 8,000 bomblets in less than one minute at ranges of up to 32 kilometres (20 miles). Other MLRS munitions include the Extended Range Rocket which, with a range of up to 45 kilometres (28 miles), carries 518 improved bomblets; the AT2 Rocket, which dispenses twenty-eight anti-tank mines; the Reduced Range Practice Round which has a range of between 8 and 15 kilometres (5 and 9 miles); and the Army Tactical Missile System (ATACMS), which saw service during the Gulf War. The ATACMS carries 950 cricket-ball-sized M74 munitions to ranges of over 165 kilometres (102 miles). There are three further variants of the ATACMS, designated Block I, II and IIA, which are equipped with thirteen BAT sub-munitions, each comprising an unpowered glider equipped with acoustic and infra-red sensors for target detection and terminal guidance respectively. The maximum range of each variant is 140 kilometres (87 miles). A new guided munition, the GMLRS, which will have a range of 70 kilometres (43 miles) and which will be equipped with a global positioning system (GPS) and an inertial guidance system, is due to enter production in 2004.

The fire-control computer permits fire missions to be carried out manually or automatically. Co-ordinates and other instructions are received from a battery command post, target data being transmitted direct into the computer which proceeds to present the crew with a series of prompts to arms and fire a pre-selected number of rounds. Multiple fire mission sequences can be programmed and stored in the computer. Rocket reload pods are carried in a tracked support vehicle, the launcher being equipped with a boom and cable hook assembly for reloading that can be controlled by a single soldier using a portable boom control device.

For the Iraqi troops, being at the receiving end of MLRS barrages was terrifying. They called the rockets 'black rain', a term referring to the high-explosive bomblets which burst over them, showering them with white-hot metal fragments. Almost 10,000 rockets were fired by a total of 189 MLRSs. At the same time, the Iraqis were also subjected to barrages by conventional artillery that engaged targets at ranges of over 24 kilometres (15 miles). By day and night, Coalition guns pounded Iraqi positions, 'softening them up' in preparation for the advance into Kuwait.

On the night of 24 February, the Coalition ground forces began their advance. Once again, technology played its part by enabling them to do so under cover of darkness. Armoured vehicles were equipped with third-generation image intensifiers and infra-red thermal imagers incorporated into their periscopes and weapon sight systems. Commanders and drivers of vehicles wore night-vision goggles that enabled them to observe the desert around them, while infantrymen were equipped with image intensifiers fitted to their personal and crew-served weapons, allowing them to be used at night.

Image intensification is a process of enhancement of light by a factor of up to 40,000, enabling items to be observed under conditions of darkness which otherwise would be invisible to the naked eye. Having no signature, image intensifiers are passive devices used for surveillance and target acquisition, being produced in a variety of configurations which include: night-vision goggles (either helmet-mounted or strapped to the user's head with a harness), used by aircrew, drivers or personnel equipped with weapons fitted with infra-red aiming projectors; individual weapon sights, mounted on rifles, machine-guns and other weapons operated by a single man; crew-served weapon sights, mounted on anti-tank guns and similar types of weapons operated by more than one man; night observation devices, large devices employed for long-range surveillance, often with photographic or video systems attached.

In the case of hand-held or weapon-mounted devices, first-generation image intensifiers were large and heavy, while their effectiveness was considerably reduced in urban environments where street or vehicle lights and other forms of white-light illumination caused the automatic gain controls to close down. The development of second-, third- and ultimately fourth-generation devices saw a marked improvement in performance with considerable reductions in size and weight as well as less susceptibility to white light.

Thermal-imaging devices operate by detecting changes in temperature and produce graphic images sufficiently detailed that operators are able to identify objects. Thermal imagery can penetrate fire, smoke, rain and foliage, thus making it ideal for surveillance and target acquisition purposes. Like image intensifiers, thermal imagers are passive devices but are vulnerable to electronic countermeasures and can be deceived by infra-red decoys.

Leading the British 1st Armoured Division were the 4th and 7th Armoured Brigades, whose armoured regiments led the way in their Challenger 1 main battle tanks (MBT), which ultimately were credited with destroying up to 300 Iraqi tanks without suffering a single casualty from enemy action. Entering service with the British Army in 1982, the Challenger 1 was based on the Shir 2, a tank originally developed for supply to Iran during the 1970s but which was never delivered due to the Iranian revolution in 1979. Powered by a Rolls Royce Condor CV-12 1,200 brake horsepower diesel engine, with an estimated maximum range of 500 kilometres (310 miles) and giving a maximum road speed of 56 kilometres (35 miles) per hour, the Challenger was equipped with hydropneumatic suspension providing improved stability across country.

With a crew of four, its turret and hull were manufactured in Chobham ceramic and steel composite armour which provides a high level of protection against the majority of battlefield weapons, including anti-tank guided weapons equipped with high-explosive anti-tank (HEAT) warheads. Its fully stabilized main armament was the Royal Ordnance L11A5 120-mm rifled gun, firing armour-piercing fin-stabilized discarding sabot tracer (APFSDS-T) and high-explosive squash head (HESH) ammunition. Secondary armament comprised two 7.62-mm machine guns: one mounted coaxially with the main armament and the other on the commander's cupola on the turret. The Challenger was equipped with a computerized fire control system, which incorporated a laser rangefinder, and featured a thermal observation and gunnery system known by its acronym of TOGS.

Following the Gulf War, Challenger 1 was replaced in 1992 by Challenger 2, which entered service in July 1994. Although possessing the same hull and running gear as Challenger 1, it is equipped with a new type of turret featuring new thermal imaging and fire control systems and designed so that it can be further enhanced with battlefield information control and navigational systems. The commander's position features a gyrostabilized fully panoramic sight, with a laser rangefinder and thermal imager, and a day/night periscope. The gunner has a similarly equipped gyrostabilized primary sight, a coaxially mounted auxiliary sight and a day/night periscope. Both hull and turret are clad in Chobham Series 2 composite armour and use Stealth technology to reduce radar signature. The main armament features the Royal Ordnance LS30 120-mm gun developed by the Royal Armaments Research and Development Establishment (RARDE) at Fort Halstead; featuring a chromed rifled bore, it is capable of firing projectiles at far higher velocities than the L11A5 fitted to the Challenger 1 and producing greater penetration of armour. The co-axially mounted machine-gun is a McDonnell Douglas 7.62-mm electro-mechanically driven weapon with adjustable rate of fire.

Following the Challengers were the Warrior infantry combat vehicles of the armoured infantry battalions. Manufactured by GKN Sankey and designed to fight its way on to an objective or provide fire support for dismounted infantry, the Warrior entered service in 1988 and eight battalions were subsequently equipped with it. With a hull constructed of all-welded aluminium armour, the vehicle is powered by a 550 brake horsepower Perkins Condor CV-8 diesel engine with an estimated maximum range of 660 kilometres (410 miles) and giving a maximum road speed of 75 kilometres (46 miles) per hour. The steel turret is power-operated and is equipped with a 30-mm Rarden cannon, a co-axially mounted Hughes EX-34 7.62-mm calibre chain gun and two quadruple-barrelled smoke grenade dischargers. Both the commander's and gunner's cupolas are equipped with Pilkington day/night sight systems and periscopes for all-round vision when closed-down. Operated by a crew of three comprising commander, gunner and driver, the Warrior accommodates a section of eight fully equipped infantrymen who deploy from the troop compartment via a power-operated door at the rear. The vehicle is not equipped for the section to fire their weapons from it but the roof of the troop compartment is equipped with periscopes and double hatches. In addition, the vehicle features a nuclear biological and chemical (NBC) warfare protection system.

Variants of Warrior include: a command post vehicle; an artillery forward observation vehicle equipped with additional radio communications and surveillance systems; an anti-tank vehicle equipped with the Milan medium range anti-tank guided missile; and a recovery vehicle.

Leading the US Army and US Marine Corps armoured formations was the M1A1 Abrams, an improved version of the M1 MBT. Designed during the 1970s and first entering service in 1980, this highly sophisticated tank also features composite armour similar to the Chobham type used on the British Challenger. In 1988, work began on the development of depleted-uranium armour for use on the M1A1. Although such armour would add a further 2 tons to the 63-ton weight of the M1A1, having a density of two and a half times that of steel, it would provide a considerably enhanced level of protection.

Operated by a commander, gunner, loader and driver, the M1A1 is powered by a 1,500 brake horsepower Avro-Lycoming AGT-1500C gas turbine engine with an estimated range of 465 kilometres (289 miles) and a maximum road speed of 68 kilometres (42 miles) per hour. When an NBC overpressure protection system is fitted, maximum range is reduced considerably to 204 kilometres (127 miles). The tank's extensive equipment specification includes a deep-water fording kit, a position location reporting system and a digital electronic fuel control unit.

The main armament was initially a 105-mm gun but this was replaced in 1986 with the M256 120-mm smoothbore weapon developed by Rheinmetall of West Germany and capable of firing M8300 High Explosive Anti-Tank Multi-Purpose Tracer (HEAT-MP-T) and APFSDS-T, the latter including a depleted uranium penetrator providing high penetration of armour. Secondary armament comprises a co-axially mounted M240 7.62-mm machine-gun, a similar weapon for use by the loader and an M2 12.7-mm heavy machine-gun equipped with a 3× sight and located on a powered mount on the commander's cupola in the turret.

The M1A1's gunner's position is equipped with a sight system incorporating a thermal imager which displays an image of the target together with a measurement of its range, accurate to within 10 metres (33 feet), which is measured by an integral laser rangefinder. The range data is automatically transferred to a digital fire control computer which automatically produces a solution that is also based on other data including wind velocity (measured by a sensor mounted on the turret), the bend of the gun (calculated by the main armament muzzle reference system), lead angle and the cant of the vehicle (provided by a pendulum static cant sensor also located on the turret). The only data entered manually is the type of round to be fired, the temperature and barometric pressure.

The commander's position is fitted with six periscopes, giving a 360° arc of observation and a stabilized thermal viewer which provides him with a day/night surveillance capability, automatic cueing of the gunner's sight and a second fire control system which enables him personally to fire the main armament. The driver's position is equipped with three periscopes, and an image intensifying periscope for use at night or in poor visibility, giving him a 120° arc of observation when driving the vehicle with his hatch closed down.

Ammunition is stored in armoured containers separated by sliding doors from the crew compartment, which is similarly separated from the vehicle's tanks by armoured bulkheads. Protection against flash or fire within the vehicle is provided by a halon gas fire suppression system designed to activate automatically within two milliseconds. In addition, the M1A1 is also equipped with an NBC warfare protection system comprising overpressure clean-air conditioning, chemical agent detection and radioactive monitoring systems. Each member of the four-man crew is also equipped with his own NBC suit and respirator.

A total of 1,178 M1A1s, transported by sea from Europe and fitted with NBC protection systems, took part in operations during the Gulf War, together with 594 M1A1 Heavy Armour (HA) tanks fitted with depleted uranium armour. All performed very satisfactorily with a high degree of reliability, few cases of mechanical failure being reported subsequently. They were opposed by a large number of Iraqi tanks, the majority of which had been supplied by the former Soviet Union. Of these, 500 were T-72 MBTs which, in spite of some advanced features, proved no match for the M1A1 with its capability of producing accurate fire while traversing rough terrain at speed. M1A1s spearheaded US assaults on Iraqi lines of defence, engaging enemy tanks at ranges of up to 4,000 metres (13,123 feet) primarily with APFSDS ammunition. The Iraqis were more often than not dug in to reduce their signature and this reduction in mobility resulted in almost 50 per cent of their number being knocked out by aircraft before Coalition forces had even crossed the border into

Kuwait. During the war, only eighteen M1A1s were withdrawn from service due to battle damage and nine suffered damage from mines; all were repairable.

During the same year as the Gulf War, the first M1A2 was delivered to the US Army. An initial fifteen M1A2s were built, followed by sixty-two. Thereafter the Pentagon placed orders for the upgrading of approximately 1,000 M1s to M1A2 configuration. Meanwhile, Saudi Arabia and Kuwait ordered 315 and 218 M1A2s respectively.

Although armed with the same 120-mm smoothbore gun as the M1A1, the M1A2 is equipped with enhanced navigation, surveillance and fire control systems. It is envisaged that ultimately all M1A2s will probably be fitted with depleted uranium armour. In addition, a further upgrading, called the System Enhancement Programme (SEP), has been introduced to enhance the M1A2's capabilities even further. This essentially comprises an upgrade to the tank's computer system, providing an operating system designed to allow further future enhancement, improved processors, increased memory capacity, high resolution colour flat-panel displays and an increased degree of user-friendliness via a soldier–machine interface. A major enhancement is the integration of a second-generation forward-looking infra-red (FLIR) sight which will replace the existing thermal imager system and the commander's thermal viewer. A fully integrated variable power (3× to 6× wide field and 13×, 25× or 50× narrow field) target acquisition/sighting system, it is designed to enable both the gunner and commander to acquire and engage targets more swiftly and with greater accuracy.

Other SEP enhancements include an under-armour auxiliary power unit capable of producing all the electrical and hydraulic power required during surveillance operations, when the tank's main engine is switched off, and of charging the vehicle's batteries. In addition, a thermal management system has also been included; this ensures that the temperature within the crew compartment is maintained under 95° and that of electronic units under 125°, ensuring maximum operability in extreme conditions.

Like its British counterpart, the Warrior, the M2 Bradley Infantry Fighting Vehicle is designed to provide mobile protection for armoured infantry and fire support for dismounted operations. It features a hull manufactured from welded aluminium reinforced in certain areas with spaced laminate armour. Operated by a crew of three – commander, gunner and driver – it carries a six-man infantry section in its troop compartment in the rear from which weapons can be used via firing ports in the hull. Designed to keep up with the M1A1/M1A2 Abrams MBT, the Bradley is powered by a Cummins VTA-903T 600 brake horsepower turbo-diesel engine with a maximum range of 483 kilometres (300 miles) and giving a maximum speed of 66 kilometres (41 miles) per hour. The vehicle is amphibious, being equipped with an inflatable pontoon fitting to the front and sides of the vehicle with propulsion, at a speed of just over 6 kilometres (4 miles) per hour being provided by the tracks.

The vehicle's main armament is the McDonnell Douglas M242 Bushmaster 25-mm chain gun which is capable of firing either armour-piercing (AP) or high-explosive (HE) ammunition, selection of either being available via operation of a switch. Capable of defeating the majority of armoured vehicles, including some MBTs, the Bushmaster has a maximum range of 2,000 metres

(6,560 feet), depending on the type of ammunition in use, and can be fired either semi-automatically or automatically. The standard rate of fire is 200 rounds per minute. Mounted coaxially is an M240 7.62-mm machine-gun.

For dealing with heavy armour, the M2A1 version of the Bradley is equipped with two TOW anti-tank guided missiles carried in a housing on the left-hand side of the turret. Reaching a speed of almost Mach 1 during flight, the highly accurate TOW is equipped with a large shaped-charge high-explosive warhead reportedly capable of destroying any known armoured vehicle. Launching of the missile, however, has to be carried out while the vehicle is stationary, and the reloading of the launcher housing is carried out by the infantry section in the rear of the vehicle via a special hatch.

A variant of the M2A1 version is the M3 Bradley Cavalry Fighting Vehicle which differs externally from the M2 in only one way – the absence of firing ports in the hull. With the familiar crew of three (commander, gunner and driver), the M3 carries two scouts, additional radio communications equipment and either Tube-launched, Optically tracked, Wire-guided (TOW) or Dragon missiles.

During the Gulf War, a total of 2,200 Bradleys were deployed in Saudi Arabia and Kuwait. Acting in close concert with US Army tank units, they followed up close behind and engaged Iraqi infantry and armour. According to one report, more enemy armoured vehicles were destroyed by Bradleys than by M1A1 MBTs. Tragically, however, some fell victim to friendly fire by US aircraft which attacked and destroyed a number of vehicles.

Following the Gulf War, upgraded versions of both vehicles were developed and produced. The M2A2 featured additional appliqué, steel armour to enhance ballistic protection, with provisions being made for the use of explosive reactive armour tiles designed to defeat shaped charge warheads. Subsequent developments resulted in the A3 upgrade which included a vehicle control and operation system designed to control and automate some crew functions and to enable transmission, reception, storage and display of digital data; an improved target acquisition and engagement system and an independent thermal viewer for the commander, both second-generation FLIR; and a GPS satellite navigation system.

Although the opening phase of the Gulf War was conducted by the Coalition air forces, the very first shots were fired by a unit of the US Army. In the early hours of 17 January 1991 two USAF MF-53J Pave Low III special operations helicopters, newly equipped with satellite navigation systems, guided eight AH-64A Apache attack helicopters of the 101st Airborne Division (Air Assault) towards the Saudi border and two key Iraqi air defence radar sites. Shortly afterwards, the Apaches attacked both installations with Hellfire missiles, destroying them both and punching a large hole 32 kilometres (20 miles) wide in the Iraqi air defence system, enabling Coalition aircraft to carry out their bombing raids deep inside Iraq.

A total of 274 Apaches were deployed during the Gulf War. Before the start of ground operations, they attacked enemy armoured units while also carrying out reconnaissance and attack missions deep into Iraqi-held territory. Once Coalition forces advanced into Kuwait, Apaches provided close air support against Iraqi armour, ultimately being credited with destroying over 500 tanks and hundreds of armoured personnel carriers and soft-skinned vehicles.

Introduced into US Army service in 1984, the Apache is a multi-role combat helicopter designed to operate by day and night, and in adverse weather conditions. Powered by two General Electric T700-701C turboshafts giving a cruise airspeed of 233 kilometres (145 miles) per hour, it has a combat radius of 261 kilometres (162 miles) and a flight endurance of an hour and 48 minutes which can be extended by the use of an external 1,044-litre (230-gallon) fuel tank. It is flown by a team of two positioned in tandem, the pilot's position being located behind that of the co-pilot/gunner.

With an all-metal semi-monocoque fuselage, the aircraft is designed with maximum survivability and crashworthiness in mind. The crew compartment and other vital areas are protected with armour manufactured from boron carbide bonded with Kevlar which provides protection against weapons up to 12.7-mm calibre. Blast shields, which provide ballistic protection against weapons up to 23-mm calibre, act as bulkheads between the pilot and co-pilot's positions, thus ensuring that at least one will survive a strike by a single round.

Nicknamed the 'Flying Tank', the Apache is equipped with a formidable array of weapons controlled by the Target Acquisition Designation Sight (TADS) system which allows the co-pilot/gunner to acquire and engage targets by day and night and in adverse weather. Mounted in a turret in the nose of the aircraft, the TADS system comprises a day TV system fitted with a zoom lens, a forward looking infrared (FLIR) unit, a direct view optic (DVO) sight unit providing wide (18°) and narrow (3.5°) fields of view, a laser spot tracker and a laser rangefinder/designator (LRF/D). Mounted in its own turret above the nose is the Pilot Night

Vision Sensor (PNVS) which enables the pilot to fly the aircraft in all conditions.

Both TADS and PNVS are interfaced with the Integrated Helmet And Display Sighting System (IHADSS) which projects images on to 50-millimetre (2-inch) square monocular displays mounted on the crew's helmets. In the case of the pilot, key flight data, such as airspeed, radar altitude and heading, is superimposed on to data from the PNVS FLIR. To acquire and designate a target, the co-pilot/gunner merely has to observe a target, place the graticule in his helmet-mounted display on it, select a weapon and fire. The system is designed so that the pilot and co-pilot/gunner can interchange images, both being able to fire weapons and, in the case of the pilot being wounded or killed, the co-pilot/gunner being able to fly the aircraft.

First among the Apache's weapons is the McDonnell Douglas M230 30-mm chain gun, located under the aircraft's nose, which can be used against troops, soft-skinned vehicles and area targets. With a rate of fire of 625 rounds per minute and a range of 6,005 metres (19,700 feet), it fires both M789 high-explosive dual-purpose (HEDP) and M799 high-explosive incendiary (HEI) ammunition. The same types of targets can also be engaged with the Apache's Hydra-70 70-mm unguided rockets, seventy-six of which are carried in four M261 launchers mounted on four pylons located in pairs on either side of the fuselage. With a maximum range of 5.5 kilometres (nearly 3½ miles), the Hydra-70 can be fitted with different types of warhead ranging from the M151 High Explosive, for use against personnel, to the M261 High Explosive Sub-Munition, containing nine M73 sub-munitions designed for attacking light armoured or soft-skinned vehicles.

The Apache's foremost anti-armour weapon is, however, the laser-guided AGM-114 Hellfire missile, equipped with a hollow charge warhead, of which the AGM-114C, AGM-114F and AGM-114K versions are currently in service. The AGM-114C features an improved semi-active laser seeker while the AGM-114F is designed for use against reactive armour, having dual warheads. The AGM-114K Hellfire II missile also features an advanced dual warhead system, electro-optical countermeasures hardening, reprogrammability for adaptation to different threats and mission requirements, a semi-active laser seeker, an improved target reacquisition system to recover laser lock-on if lost, and a programmable autopilot for trajectory adjustment.

Once fired, Hellfire missiles can be controlled either from the launching aircraft or 'handed off' either to another aircraft or to forward observers on the ground equipped with a laser target designator which illuminates the target and guides the missile to it. The latter method has the advantage of allowing the aircraft either to remain concealed by terrain or depart the area immediately after launching a missile.

The current most advanced version of the Apache is the AH-64D Longbow Apache, a remanufactured and upgraded aircraft which features a number of enhancements which include: updated T700-701C engines, a fully integrated cockpit, digital communications, integrated GPS/inertial navigation unit, enhanced doppler velocity rate sensor, a fire control radar target acquisition system and the fire-and-forget AGM-114L Longbow version of the Hellfire missile.

The AN/APG-78 fire control radar (FCR) is a multi-mode millimetre wave sensor with its antenna and transmitter mounted on the aircraft's main rotor head. It is capable of detecting, classifying and prioritizing targets on the ground and in the air. In addition, the FCR will detect obstacles and provides assistance to the air crew when flying in adverse weather conditions. The FCR can be operated by either the co-pilot/gunner or the pilot, the latter for example using it to search for airborne targets while the other uses TADS to engage others on the ground. The system can also be used in conjunction with TADS, whose electro-optics can be used to identify targets detected by the radar. The FCR also has a threat detection capability through its Radio Frequency Interferometer (RFI) which detects and pinpoints with a high degree of accuracy radars in the search and acquisition mode, in particular when they have locked on to the Apache. The RFI contains a extensive 'library' of pre-programmed threat signatures which enables it to recognize the type of radar and weapon system threatening the aircraft.

The AGM-114L Longbow Hellfire RF missile initially accepts targeting data from the FCR but will thereafter respond to guidance from the co-pilot/gunner's TADS or from another aircraft. It is capable of operating in two modes: lock-on before launch, which is used to acquire static or mobile targets at short range prior to launching; or lock-on after launch, in which the missile acquires and locks on to stationary targets at extended ranges shortly after leaving the aircraft.

The Longbow Apache also has the capability of carrying air-to-air missiles for engagement of air targets. At the time of writing, trials are currently being conducted by the US Army with two missiles: the Raytheon Air-to-Air (ATAS) Stinger and the Shorts Starstreak. The ATAS Stinger is an infra-red homing fire-and-forget missile based on the well-proven man-portable, shoulder-fired surface-to-air missile (SAM) designed to engage aircraft at low altitudes. It is equipped with a super-cooled, two-colour passive infra-red seeker which is extremely sensitive to both infra-red and ultra-violet wavelengths, giving it the ability to avoid electrical and optical countermeasures. Also possessing an IFF system, the ATAS Stinger has enhanced range and manoeuvrability and an all-aspect engagement capability.

The Shorts Starstreak undergoing trials is a helicopter-launched version of the man-portable shoulder-fired close-range SAM designed to provide defence against helicopters and ground attack aircraft. The missile comprises a two-stage solid-propellant rocket motor, a separation system and a forward unit containing three high-density darts. Each of the latter is equipped with a thermal battery, guidance and control system, steering fins and a high-density penetrating warhead. On firing, the missile is boosted clear of the launcher by the rocket motor's initial stage which separates as the second stage ignites, the missile accelerating away and reaching a speed of over Mach 4. Canted nozzles cause the missile to roll, resulting in the deployment of stabilizing fins that provide aerodynamic stability in flight. As the second stage burns out, the three darts are automatically detached and separate, their individual warheads being armed in the process, maintaining a high degree of kinetic energy as they home in on the target. They are guided independently by a laser beam transmitted by the auto-tracker in the Apache's TADS, which scans the target in the form of a grid, the darts homing in on the geometric centre. A delay fuse is initiated as each dart impacts, allowing it to penetrate the target before exploding.

During the Gulf War, much of the target data for Coalition air, ground and naval forces was supplied by remotely piloted vehicles (RPVs), alternatively known as unmanned aerial vehicles (UAVs). These carried out a total of 522 sorties, lasting 1,641 hours, before and during Operation Desert Storm itself.

The principal RPV used by US forces in the Gulf War was the Pioneer. Initially developed in Israel and manufactured in the United States, it weighs 210.45 kilograms (463 pounds) and is 4.3 metres (14 feet) in length. Launched by pneumatic catapult and powered by a 26-horsepower two-stroke twin-cylinder rear-mounted engine running on 100-octane aviation fuel, it has a range of approximately 160 kilometres (100 miles) and a flight duration of five hours. Equipped with auto-pilot, navigation and radio-link data communications systems that enable it to operate in either programmed or manual control modes, it carries a number of high quality video sensors for conducting reconnaissance and surveillance tasks in adverse environments and under battlefield conditions. These comprise gyro-stabilized high resolution television and FLIR systems for operations during the day or at night, or in conditions of reduced visibility.

The Pioneer is controlled by a ground control station (GCS), either ship-borne or land-based, which directs it throughout the duration of a mission. Incorporating advanced electronics for mission planning and execution, the GCS comprises three bays manned by two operators: the Pilot Bay contains all the controls and displays necessary for control of the RPV; the Observer Bay provides control facilities for all the on-board sensors; and the Tracking Bay displays the RPV's location based on data provided by a tracking communication unit (TCU). Located separately from the GCS, the TCU contains a communications system providing a highly sophisticated jam-resistant data link, with a range of 169 kilometres (100 miles), for both control of the RPV and for real-time downlink of video and telemetry transmissions from the on-board sensors. In a land-based system, the TCU can be remotely located up to 1,000 metres (3,280 feet) from the GCS, being connected with the latter via a fibre-optic link.

During the preflight, launch and recovery stages of a mission, a portable control station can be used by the pilot to control the RPV, enabling the GCS to concentrate on other tasks. In order to enable commanders in the field to receive immediate results of an aerial reconnaissance of areas of operations, remote receiving stations can be located at their headquarters, providing them with the most up-to-date information.

The Pioneer saw shipborne service during the Gulf War with the US Navy, and on land with US Army and US Marine Corps units. RPVs were launched from the battleships USS *Missouri* and USS *Wisconsin*, proving highly successful in the roles of target selection, gunfire support, battle damage assessment and maritime interception operations. In the case of the latter, two Iraqi high-speed craft were intercepted and destroyed as a result of information provided by a Pioneer. In the surveillance role, Pioneers pinpointed Iraqi coastal surface-to-surface missile batteries and air defence batteries, as well as identifying over 300 vessels and detecting movements by major Iraqi armoured formations. They flew a total of sixty-four sorties lasting 213 hours, providing support for naval gunfire in a total of eighty-three fire missions.

On shore, a US Army UAV platoon was assigned to VII Corps and its Pioneers proved invaluable in flying a total of forty-six sorties over 155 flying hours during which they sent back video coverage of a large number of targets including enemy armour, artillery, convoys, fortifications and command posts. Such were the numbers of targets identified that there were simply too many to be engaged rapidly enough.

Three US Marine Corps UAV companies were deployed during the Gulf War and their Pioneers were used in the reconnaissance, surveillance and target acquisition (RSTA) role. Once targets such as troops, armour, artillery, surface-to-air missile (SAM) sites, bunkers and supply depots had been located and identified, the information was used for directing gunfire or close air support on to them. Such was the quality of the material transmitted by the Pioneers that on one occasion a SAM site was not attacked as the video clearly showed that it was a dummy. During the entire war, US Marine Pioneers flew 323 missions during a total of 980 flying hours.

Such was the success of the Pioneer during the Gulf War that it was deployed aboard US Navy warships on operations during the mid-1990s in Haiti, Somalia and Bosnia. In the case of Bosnia, a Pioneer was launched on 13 October 1995 from the US Navy amphibious assault ship USS *Shreveport* to conduct an examination of the damage caused by Serb shelling of Mostar where a United Nations safe-haven was located. Thereafter, it carried out reconnaissance missions in which it gathered intelligence on the state of roads, bridges, tunnels and villages which had been reported as badly damaged by shelling. The Pioneer was able to show that much damage had been repaired and that roads and bridges were once again operational. A similar mission was carried out over the port of Dubrovnik and towns further inland on the following day.

The featureless desert terrain over which the Coalition forces advanced and fought during Operation Desert Storm was such that maps were of little use in navigating over the sandy wastes. The difficulties facing commanders of vehicles and units are well illustrated by one British artillery officer when describing his own experience of the high speed advance into Kuwait: 'You've got to imagine from the point of view of my job: you're in a vehicle bumping up and down, you've got the flat featureless terrain, you've got your headsets on with your infantry commander talking in one ear and your artillery commander speaking in the other – it is very hard to cope with all that and read a map as well.'

The key to troops navigating accurately around the desert lay in the fact that the heavens are criss-crossed by a network of satellites forming the Global Positioning System (GPS). Each satellite broadcasts a continuous signal, giving the time and its precise position, which is picked up by receivers installed in ships, vehicles and aircraft, or hand-held by personnel, which use it to calculate their respective positions on or above the Earth's surface.

Operation Desert Storm was the first large-scale operational military use of GPS and it proved invaluable. Not only were commanders of armoured formations able to navigate accurately during the day and at night while moving at speed, and to report their locations when required to do so, but logistic support units, bringing up fuel, ammunition and rations, were also able to rendezvous with the desert with frontline units. As Lieutenant Colonel Peter Williams of the Royal Artillery later commented, 'Certainly,

I ignored my maps, threw them away and relied totally on my satellite navigation device. It was such a brilliant system which enabled us not only to determine where we were at any given time but also to key in where we wanted to go. If we wanted to put in any waypoints, it would actually navigate for us – it would say left a bit, right a bit, the whole way there. The only trouble was, very occasionally, for about half an hour in the morning and evening the satellites would obviously be out of orientation and you would get a dreaded display saying "GPS bad" – gloom all round because it meant that it wasn't going to tell you where you were and wasn't going to help you at all. So, the show tended to grind to a halt during those periods.'

There is currently more than one GPS system in operation. The one developed by the US Department of Defense, during the eighteen years prior to the Gulf War, is called Navstar and comprises two segments: Space and Control. The Space Segment nominally comprises a constellation of twenty-four satellites that orbit the earth over a period of twelve hours, repeating the same track and configuration over any point approximately every twenty-four hours. There are six orbital planes, with four satellites in each, equally spaced 60° apart and inclined at approximately 55° to the equator. Between five and eight satellites are visible from any location on the Earth's surface at any one time.

The Control Segment, called the Operational Control System, comprises a master control station (MCS) located at Schriever Air Force Base near Colorado Springs, where it is operated by the USAF's 2nd Space Operations Squadron, and a network of five passive monitoring stations. The first of these is also located near Colorado Springs, the other four being on the islands of Hawaii, Ascension Island in the South Atlantic, Diego Garcia in the Indian Ocean and Kwajalein in the Pacific. These track the satellites twenty-four hours a day, passing real-time data to the MCS which analyses it to determine whether there have been any changes or malfunctions. Any navigational or other instructions from the MCS are transmitted once or twice a day by radio to the satellites via three ground-based uplink antenna systems located on Ascension Island, Diego Garcia and Kwajalein.

The Navstar system provides two services. The Precise Positioning Service (PPS) is available only to US and Allied military forces, and authorized civilian agencies. These organizations are equipped with the necessary cryptographic systems and keys necessary to decode the signals which provide a degree of accuracy of 22 metres (72 feet) horizontally and just under 28 metres (92 feet) vertically. Other civilian users have access to the Standard Positioning Service (SPS), which is available worldwide at no cost to the user and without restrictions. Intentionally degraded by the US Department of Defense, SPS provides a degree of accuracy of only 100 metres (328 feet) horizontally and 156 (510 feet) metres vertically.

The Gulf War was the first major conflict that saw extensive use of high technology. On the Coalition side, computers were used at all levels, ranging from hand-held devices computing mortar fire data to the highly sophisticated systems in Washington and London being fed with up-to-date intelligence information to produce 'game plan' scenarios and proposed solutions. In the final analysis, however, it was always the senior commanders who had to take decisions.

As General Sir Peter de la Billière, commander of British forces during the Gulf War, later stated: 'The computer feed-outs that we then had were obviously information that we looked at very carefully and considered. But let's be quite clear, computers don't run wars – human beings run wars and you must be very careful to make sure that all the information you get from computers is no more than just another piece of information. At the end of the day, you the commander have got to take the decisions and make judgements based on a wide range of information, including that provided by computers.'

DAWN OF THE DEATH RAY

Despite the end of the Cold War and the current programmes of partial nuclear disarmament being
conducted by the United States and Russia, there is still a
potential threat from ballistic missiles in certain regions.
Although reduced in size, Russia's intercontinental ballistic
missile (ICBM) arsenal still poses a major threat to the West,
and it is estimated that by 2015 it will still possess as many
missiles as its economy will permit, albeit well within the
limitations laid down by the START treaties. Furthermore,
China will by that time probably possess small but significant quantities of ICBMs capable of reaching the West.

In September 1999 the US National Intelligence
Council's Office for Strategic and Nuclear Programmes produced a report outlining emerging ballistic missile threats
in other regions. Foremost among those nations believed to
be capable of producing ICBMs within the next fifteen years
is North Korea, whose Taepo Dong 2 space launch vehicle
reportedly could be converted to an ICBM capable of carrying a warhead payload of several hundred kilograms with
sufficient range to reach the United States. Similarly, the
report states that Iran, with Russian assistance and technology, could test a North Korean type ICBM, capable of
delivering a payload of several hundred kilograms to some

parts of the United States, by the end of this decade. Likewise, Iraq is reported as possibly being able to test a similar weapon by 2010 although this would depend on the degree of foreign assistance available.

Meanwhile, in southern Asia and elsewhere in the Middle East there has been a proliferation of short-range (SRBM) and medium-range (MRBM) ballistic missiles with maximum ranges of under 1,000 kilometres (621 miles) and 1,000 to 3,000 kilometres (621 to 1,864 miles) respectively. Pakistan possesses M-11 SRBMs and Ghauri MRBMs, both supplied by North Korea, while India has developed its Prithvi SRBM and is currently testing the Agni MRBM. In May 2000, it was reported that Syria had purchased 300 Scud-D SRBMs and twenty-six mobile launchers from North Korea. With a range of 708 kilometres (440 miles), this weapon would enable the Syrians to hit all areas of Israel from deep within their own territory.

Such weapons could inflict considerable damage on Western forces or interests, as was illustrated in 1991 during the Gulf War when Iraq launched its Scud missiles against Coalition forces and Israel. According to the National Intelligence Council report, missiles with conventional high explosive have been used in a number of regional conflicts during the last twenty years.

It is for these reasons that the United States in particular is developing new defensive weapon systems, based on powerful high-energy lasers, to counter the ballistic missile threat not only within the continental United States but in areas where US and Western interests or forces come under threat.

History has it that the first recorded use of light on the battlefield occurred over 2,000 years ago during the Peloponnesian Wars in ancient Greece when troops on one side used the concave faces of their highly polished bronze shields to direct the rays of the sun into the eyes of the enemy. The story goes that such was the painfully dazzling effect of the concentrated mass of light that victory was assured at a stroke.

At its focal pinpoint, laser light is capable of an intensity greater than that of the sun and can unleash terrifying force. One example is a laser developed in the United States, the most powerful of its type in the world, which produces a beam whose power is officially secret but reportedly is several times greater than the temperature on the surface of the sun (about 5,500°C).

One of the earliest attempts in the development of laser weapons began during the late 1960s in the United States, at Kirtland Air Force Base in the deserts of New Mexico. The experimental high-energy laser weighed over 30 tons and required a crew of four to aim and fire it. The size of the weapon was massive, its huge fuel tanks and optics covering half an acre, the largest of its optics being a tracking telescope used to aim the beam. The first breakthrough came in November 1973 during trials against moving targets with the laser engaging a drone (an unmanned, remotely piloted aircraft) flying a 'racetrack' pattern around the test area. During the first test, the drone cut a corner and consequently caused a nearby steel weather tower to be aligned briefly between the aircraft and the laser tracking it. Since the tracking was effected by infra-red energy, the beam locked on to the top of the tower as a hotter target than the drone and melted the structure.

A second test brought more success. Another drone was launched and flown along a valley approximately 1.5 kilometres (nearly a mile) away from the base. At that distance, the 3.7-metre (12-foot) long aircraft was merely a small dot in the sky but the beam locked on to the heat emitted by the drone's engine and in just over a second burned a hole in the steel fuselage immediately below the wing. The fuel tank exploded and the drone broke up, the reusable engine unit descending on a small parachute and landing some 300 metres (985 feet) from the wreckage of the fuselage. This test had proved that the concept of a system reaching out at the speed of light and destroying a missile or aircraft was feasible. The problem in those early days, however, was the huge size and immensely high cost of such a weapon.

A high-energy laser comprises a glass tube filled with gas. The atoms that make up the gas are bombarded with electricity, 'exciting' them so that they emit light waves. At each end of the laser is a mirror that some light waves, travelling in harmony, bounce off and so head back into the gas, forcing other already excited atoms to release more light. As an increasing number of atoms are forced to release light, powerful light waves build up inside the gas and eventually burst through one of the mirrors. The amplified light waves are by then in perfect harmony, forming a laser beam. By injecting more energy to create an increased number of excited atoms, the beam's power is increased. As the energy input is stepped up, so the device that contains it must also grow.

Most early high-energy lasers grew so large that they never left the laboratories in which they were constructed. The team conducting experiments at Kirtland during the 1970s encountered the fundamental dilemma facing those attempting to build such weapons: the smaller the laser, the less power it possesses. However, the scientists at Kirtland not only were determined to overcome this problem but had also conceived a highly ambitious plan to put a high-energy laser on an airborne platform.

In 1973 an NKC-135A aircraft, one of fourteen USAF KC-135As permanently modified for special test projects, arrived at Kirtland Air Force Base where a high-energy laser was installed in it; the only indication of the aircraft's special role was a large 'hump' on its back. It was to serve as an airborne laser laboratory (ALL) containing a fully operational gas dynamic 500,000-watt laser built at a cost of 31.2 million dollars. On emission from the laser, the beam was relayed via a series of mirrors up to the telescope in the hump of the aircraft and fired from a turret with a power of 0.38 megawatts.

In October 1980 the ALL carried out its maiden flight; the laser system was so heavy that the aircraft could carry only enough fuel for four hours of flying, the KC-135's normal endurance being considerably more. There was some dangerous chemistry aboard the ALL. Hot carbon dioxide and nitrogen gases were blasted into a low pressure chamber where they expanded rapidly, releasing their energy as light, to form the beam. The fuels for the laser system, nitrogen and an oxidizer, were contained in liquid form in pressurized tanks. Not only were they also hazardous but helium gas, used to force the reactants from the storage tanks into the combustors, was stored in another tank at a pressure of 6,000 pounds per square inch (422 kilograms per square centimetre). The aircraft would have been destroyed in an instant if the tank had exploded through pressure.

Moreover, the laser beam itself proved to pose a hazard, this becoming apparent when burn marks appeared on panels inside the aircraft. Investigation of these revealed that what looked like sparks were in fact dust particles that had been caught in the path of the beam. The sides of the particles exposed to the beam vaporized, imparting them with momentum like miniature rocket engines. If the hurtling particles did not disintegrate, there was a risk of their striking the laser's sensitive optics. Furthermore, if one was ignited it could cause a sparkle effect, interfering with the beam sensors. The solutions to this problem were to ensure that the atmosphere within the laser compartment of the ALL was of clean-room air quality and to reduce the sensitivity of the beam sensors to the spectrum of the exploding dust while at the same time increasing their sensitivity to the laser radiation by the introduction of a narrow band filter.

After a few years of experiments, the ALL began a series of trials to discover whether it could intercept an AIM-9 Sidewinder air-to-air missile travelling at over 3,200 kilometres (2,000 miles) per hour. There was only one way to conduct such tests: the ALL itself would have to act as a target for the missile launched by an aircraft. In the event of the ALL being hit, it would be destroyed. There was only one safety precaution that could be taken: the missile was equipped with insufficient fuel to reach the ALL. However, there was a possibility that if the launching aircraft pitched upwards as it launched the Sidewinder, then there would be sufficient energy in the missile to arc over and head towards the ALL.

Just such a course of events did indeed take place on one occasion during the trials, and the members of the crew aboard the ALL could do nothing but watch as the missile headed directly towards the aircraft. It came close enough for them to see its fins but fortunately it ran out of fuel at the very last moment and dropped away, to the great relief of all concerned. The event was later recalled by Colonel John Otten, a member of the crew and the officer in charge of the test flights: 'Our chase airplane, the man who was flying with us and watching what was happening, disappeared. He was history. Our airplane was not getting out of the way of anything. We sat quietly and watched this missile come in toward us, and on the screen, you could see it coming toward you and it got big enough to where you could see the fins on it, you could actually see them start to wiggle. And then it dropped out and went away. Everybody was a little excited.'

It took three years before the ALL succeeded in destroying a missile, by which time the USAF was becoming impatient and time was running out. On 26 May 1983 it scored its first hit, the first of five in which the laser beam fractured the nose of the Sidewinder, breaking the homing lock and causing the missile to go off target. During the following autumn, the ALL succeeded in intercepting two US Navy BQM-34A Firebee drones representing sea-skimming cruise missiles. In each case the laser beam, from a range of over 1.5 kilometres (about a mile), struck the drones' flight control boxes and sent them diving into the sea.

While the system had proved capable of intercepting missiles, the trials had highlighted its limited range. Maximum effective range was achieved at night, while in daylight, with good weather, it was reduced to only a few miles beyond which atmospheric particles disrupted the laser beam. As a result of this limitation, the USAF decided the system was not an effective missile interceptor and in the mid-1980s the ALL was mothballed. It appeared that the dream of airborne laser air defence was over.

Elsewhere, however, even greater ambitions were being pursued. In the early 1980s, despite progress with arms control treaties, the threat of nuclear conflict was still very real. If a missile was launched from a Soviet silo or submarine, it was almost impossible to intercept during the flight to its target. But there were some scientists who still believed that there was a way of utilizing the power of the laser in space. Although it seemed very ambitious, there was a logical reason that led them to believe that a space-based laser would succeed where its airborne predecessor had failed. Whereas the latter has to shoot through the Earth's atmosphere, even when thin at high altitudes, a space-based laser has the advantage of being outside the atmosphere where there is nothing to penetrate. In essence, space is an ideal environment for a laser to operate.

From March 1983 onwards, President Ronald Reagan allocated up to 3 billion dollars per year to develop and build a space-based laser system designed to provide a defensive shield against nuclear ballistic missile attacks from within the Soviet Union. Popularly known as 'Star Wars', it was officially designated the Strategic Defence Initiative (SDI). The idea was to put a series of lasers on platforms in orbit around the Earth, at appropriate altitudes, which provided twenty-four-hour continuous coverage of the surface of the planet. If a missile was fired by a belligerent nation, it could be intercepted with a laser beam from a range of thousands of miles and destroyed as it broke through the clouds.

This sounded fine in theory but in practice, as far as most scientists were concerned, it was in the realms of science fiction. In order to intercept a missile in its boost phase, before it launches decoys, the laser would have to strike from a range of up to 8,000 kilometres (5,000 miles) which would require high-precision aiming. Furthermore, the accuracy of lasers had never been tested in space.

The only system designed to test the capabilities of a space-based laser is Alpha, developed by TRW Space & Electronics Group at its Capistrano Test Site. It is a system producing a beam approximately 30 centimetres (12 inches) in diameter and over a million watts in power which would have a range of 8,000 kilometres (5,000 miles) in the vacuum of space. This is generated by a mixture of deuterium, nitrogen trifluoride and helium producing fluorine, which is then burned with hydrogen in a mirrored chamber known as an optical resonator. This process creates hydrogen fluoride molecules which become excited before returning to a calm state, at which point they emit a cascade of photons that are amplified and converted into a beam. The beam-control system, comprising an assembly of optics and mirrors, magnifies the beam and directs it at its target.

Alpha was constructed during the 1980s but was not fired until 1989. By the beginning of the 1990s, by which time its total cost had reached 45 billion dollars, the SDI programme had not even produced a prototype. The Pentagon was swiftly becoming disenchanted and was beginning to think that the SDI scientists were on a wild goose chase. In 1993 the programme was shelved.

During the next five years, however, Alpha was fired twelve more times with a five-second full-power test firing taking place on 18 September 1996. Revival of the concept of ballistic missile defence took place that same year with the introduction of the Defend America Act which recognized the growing threat of ballistic missile proliferation and aimed to establish policy for the eventual development and deployment of a missile defence system covering the entire nation. During the following year, the United States and Russia agreed on a reinterpretation of the Anti-Ballistic

Missile Treaty of 1972, this resulting in the lifting of a ban on lasers and missile-based systems subject to certain limitations. Subsequently, approval was given for further development of Alpha, with a successful five-second test firing taking place in September 1996 and another during the following year. The latest known test-firing of Alpha took place in March 2000 when a six-second test resulted in a 25 per cent increase in power output and beam quality.

Under the auspices of the Ballistic Missile Defence Organization (BMDO), the revived concept, with a projected cost of 80 billion dollars, envisages up to twenty satellites, each carrying a deuterium-fluoride chemical SBL and weighing 35,000 kilograms (15,900 pounds), orbiting on platforms 800 to 1,300 kilometres (500 to 800 miles) above the Earth's surface and engaging missiles as they climb in boost phase to a point just outside the atmosphere. Each laser would possess sufficient capacity to engage up to 100 missiles at a range of up to 4,000 kilometres (2,500 miles), taking less than ten seconds to do so and only one second to switch between targets. If the programme keeps to schedule, a half-scale prototype, weighing 17,500 kilograms (38,500 pounds) and costing 1.5 billion dollars, will be launched into space via a Titan-4 missile between the years 2005 and 2008; an operational system comprising six high-energy space-borne lasers (SBL) is reportedly scheduled to be in operation by the end of 2010.

Meanwhile, prior to the revival of Star Wars, a new initiative to find a viable solution to the threat of Theatre Ballistic Missiles (TBMs) had been launched under the auspices of the Strategic Defence Initiative Organization (SDIO) which, through its previous involvement in the development of global missile defence systems, was already familiar with laser technology. In November 1991 the director of the SDIO initiated the first studies into the new concept of installing a high-energy laser on an airborne platform to intercept TBMs at long range. In August 1992, recommendations were given for the development of an Airborne Laser (ABL) prototype. Shortly afterwards, responsibility for the new development programme was transferred from the SDIO to the USAF. This time, the idea was to install a high-energy laser on a large aircraft for operation at very high altitudes where it would be unaffected by weather while still having time to intercept missiles during their boost stages.

The result was a chemical oxygen iodine laser (COIL) which produces light as a result of a chemical reaction: excited oxygen atoms are extracted from reacting hydrogen peroxide and chlorine and then pumped into iodine gas to generate a massive burst of energy which the iodine atoms release as an intense beam of laser light. Invented at the Phillips Laboratory at Kirtland Air Force Base in 1977, its principal advantage is that, unlike earlier lasers, it does not require a large power plant, being powered by a fuel comprising hydrogen peroxide and potassium hydroxide which are then combined with chlorine gas and water. Furthermore, its infra-red wavelength is only 1.315 microns, the shortest in the world for a high-powered laser. This wavelength travels through the atmosphere without any difficulty and has increased brightness and destructive strength when striking the target.

As described earlier, the principal limitation of the system carried on the ALL was one of range, and thus a high degree of effort was concentrated on overcoming this problem. Astronomers at Kirtland's Starfire Observatory, which tracks satellites and keeps them under surveillance, had already done so by developing an optical device that is capable of penetrating the atmosphere: a telescope, at the base of which is a mirror that bends. The device transmits a massive laser beam and any atmospheric distortion is viewed through the telescope as a shifting pattern of dots of light. A computer in the device calculates precise values for the shifts and these are relayed to tiny motors that push and pull at the mirror's surface, creating minuscule variations. The flexing in the mirror shifts the dots back to where they should be and the atmospheric distortion is reduced, improving the telescope's vision by 1,000 per cent. It was decided that a similar system would be incorporated in the new ABL laser: a flexible mirror increasing the power and range of the beam.

Meanwhile, consideration was being given to the type of platform that would carry the ABL. In September 1992 the aircraft manufacturer Boeing was awarded a contract to carry out an assessment on how well an existing large aircraft, such as a 707, 747 or even a B-52 bomber, would be suited to the role. In the event, a modified 747 proved to be the recommended airframe.

A year later a consortium of Boeing, TRW Space & Electronics Group and Lockheed Martin Missiles & Space, operating under the name Team ABL, submitted its proposals to the USAF ABL Program Office at Kirtland. With a strong history of successful management of large programmes and the development of weapon systems, Boeing offered extensive experience in integration of complex systems within aircraft through its work on programmes such as the AWACS. In addition to having designed and developed Alpha, TRW had considerable experience in the manufacture of lasers dating back to the late 1960s when it had developed and integrated the high-energy laser and beam control system aboard the ALL which had destroyed the Sidewinder missiles and Firebee drones in flight. Thereafter, during the early 1970s, TRW had also produced for the USAF the Mid-Infra-Red Advanced Chemical Laser (MIRACL), a megawatt-class continuous wave deuterium fluoride chemical laser. The third member of the consortium, Lockheed Martin, meanwhile had extensive experience in the development and manufacture of large-size optics and high-precision aiming systems for high-energy lasers.

In November 1996, after consideration of a competitive bid from another consortium, a 1.1 billion dollar Program Definition and Risk Reduction (PDRR) contract was awarded to Team ABL. The aim of this stage of the project was to develop a system that would prove conclusively that all the necessary technology was available. Based on a commercial 747-400F airframe, which was to be available for modification by early 1999, the prototype attack laser aircraft was to be flight tested by 2001. Designated YAL-1A, although still known as the ABL, it had to be able to demonstrate that it could intercept and destroy a missile in its 'boost' phase by the latter part of 2002. Boeing would be responsible for systems integration, airframe modification and development of battle management systems. The latter would include computers and software handling communications, intelligence, target detection and engagement. TRW would develop the laser while Lockheed Martin would be responsible for the beam and fire control systems. On successful completion of this initial contract, a further one worth approximately 4.5 billion dollars would be awarded for the engineering, manufacturing, development and production of a fleet of seven ABLs, the first three being completed by 2006 and the remaining four by 2008.

The internal configuration of the ABL has the megawatt-class high-energy laser, designed with aircraft safety and ease of field maintenance in mind, mounted in the rear half of the fuselage. Forward of that are situated two state-of-the-art diode-pumped solid-state lasers, the tracking illuminator laser (TILL) and the beacon illuminator laser (BILL), which acquire and track a target, and direct the main high-energy laser on to it. Dividing the laser compartment from the rest of the interior of the aircraft is a bulkhead equipped with an airlock, which provides controlled access to the rear of the aircraft. Forward of the bulkhead is the battle management compartment, containing modular consoles equipped with computer systems for target detection, identification, prioritization and nomination; surveillance and tracking; launch and impact point predictions; theatre interoperability; and common data/voice link communications to joint theatre assets. Mounted on the aircraft's distinctive 'hump' above the flight deck is the active laser ranger comprising a modified third-generation LANTIRN (Low Altitude Navigation and Targeting Infra-Red for Night) with a high-power gas dynamic CO_2 laser. This device acquires a target from the Infra-Red Search and Track (IRST) sensor cue, tracks it and directs the CO_2 laser for ranging, assisting in pinpointing the missile's launch and impact points.

Located forward of the battle management compartment is the beam/fire control system, which provides target acquisition and tracking, fire control engagement and sequencing, and aim point-and-kill assessment. The system also carries out high-energy laser beam wavefront control and atmospheric compensation, jitter control, alignment/beam-walk control, and beam containment for both the high-energy and illuminator lasers. It features calibration and diagnostics systems that provide autonomous real-time and post-mission analysis. Finally, on the nose of the aircraft, mounted in a turret assembly housed in a shell permitting rotation of 150° is a 150-centimetre (60-inch) telescope that focuses the laser beams on a target and collects returned images and signals. Incorporated in it is a flexible mirror, nearly 160 centimetres (62 inches) in diameter and just over 20 centimetres (8 inches) thick, equipped with 341 actuators that effect variations in the mirror's surface at the rate of approximately 1,000 per second.

The sequence of target engagement by the system would be as follows. The battle management systems provide target co-ordinates to the beam/fire control system that traverses the turret, centring the target in the acquisition sensor, acquiring the plume of the missile in the coarse track sensor. The TILL then acquires the body of the missile and actively tracks its nose. The beam control process begins after active tracking has been established by the firing of the BILL to establish the aiming point on the target for the high-energy laser. The resulting spot on the missile is imaged in the wavefront sensor and compared with the outgoing sample of the BILL. At this point, the high-energy laser is fired in a three- to five-second burst along the same path with similar wavefront correction, burning the skin of the missile's body until it ruptures and explodes.

The operational concept of the ABL is that of a rapidly deployable anti-TBM defence system which can deploy from the continental United States within a matter of hours.

Flown by crews of four and operating in pairs, ABL aircraft will fly orbits at high altitude over areas to be defended, scanning for the exhaust plumes of missiles. If missiles are launched, the ABL will detect them on passing through the clouds and destroy them, the resulting debris falling back on to enemy territory below. Given its size and lack of manoeuvrability, however, the ABL will be unable to fly over hostile territory because of its vulnerability to air and ground attack, and thus will have to engage targets at long range while flying at altitudes of around 12,000 metres (40,000 feet). The high-energy COIL laser will have a range of 300 to 600 kilometres (185 to 375 miles) but, as missiles would have to be intercepted while in the boost stage of their flight, it will only have between 40 and 100 seconds to engage and destroy its target. The ABL will be designed to possess a salvo engagement capability, capable of engaging multiple targets and carrying sufficient chemical laser fuel to destroy between twenty and forty missiles before needing to refuel.

Although capable of autonomous operations, the ABL will normally be a fully integrated element in a series of systems designed to provide missile defence in depth, destroying TBMs in the boost phase of launch.

Among other systems currently under development is the Airborne Tactical Laser (ATL), a lightweight high-energy laser designed specifically for tactical airborne or ground-based operations. Derived from the COIL system developed by TRW for the ABL, this new system is optimized for power levels of 100 to 500 kilowatts and is designed to operate at ground level with laser exhaust emissions being contained by a small sealed exhaust system.

Comprising the laser and an on-board optical sensor suite, the system will be configured in a roll-on/roll-off package for installation in aircraft, such as the AC-130 Spectre gunship, CH-47D Chinook or the V-22 Osprey, or ground vehicles. Intended for low-level below-cloud use against anti-ship or cruise missiles, the ALT will reportedly be capable of engaging targets at ranges of over 20 kilometres (12 miles) when used in the air-to-air or air-to-ground roles, and up to 10 kilometres (6 miles) in the ground-to-air role. It is envisaged that in the latter, a fully mobile ground-based system, contained in two vehicles, could be employed to counter short-range tactical rockets.

Equipped with different sensor and fire control systems, the ATL could also be used in an offensive role in special operations, carrying out precision strike tasks where pin-point accuracy and zero collateral damage are required. According to one report, the ATL laser will deliver sufficient power to place a beam on a 15-centimetre (6-inch) diameter target point and melt a metal object in a few seconds from a range of 8 kilometres (5 miles).

Also currently being developed is the tactical high energy laser (THEL), a joint programme being carried out by the US Army Space and Missile Defence Command (SMDC) and the Israeli Army under a 131-million-dollar-contract funded by both countries. Designed as a ground-based short-range missile and rocket defence system, THEL comprises a pointer/tracker that will detect, track and target multiple rocket launches; a command, control, communications and intelligence (C3I) sub-system; and a deuterium fluoride chemical laser with a reported range of 5 kilometres (3 miles) and sufficient fuel capacity for up to sixty shots before refuelling.

The concept and effectiveness of such systems against short-range missiles and rockets was first demonstrated in

1996. On 9 February of that year, a test was carried out at the High Energy Laser Systems Test Facility at the US Army SMDC's missile test range at White Sands, New Mexico, in which a rocket was destroyed in mid-air. The laser used in the test was MIRACL, the megawatt-class chemical laser built in the 1970s by TRW. One of the most powerful lasers in the United States used for defence research purposes, MIRACL has been employed in several such tests, including one in October 1997 in which it successfully hit the USAF's small MSTI-3 satellite orbiting at an altitude of 418 kilometres (260 miles) above the Earth's surface. In other tests, MIRACL successfully shot down five Firebee drones and a Vandal supersonic missile. During the February 1996 test, however, it used only a small fraction of its power, equating to that of a ground-based mobile system of the type that THEL would comprise.

Two months after the test President Bill Clinton and Secretary of Defense William J. Perry attended a meeting with the Prime Minister of Israel, Shimon Peres, at which a commitment was made that the United States would help Israel in the development of a THEL system to assist in the defence of the north of Israel against short-range rockets, such as the Russian-manufactured 122-mm Katyusha, fired by the Lebanese terrorist group Hizbollah from southern Lebanon. On 18 July, the THEL demonstrator development was formally initiated by a memorandum of agreement between the governments of the two countries. The contract for the design, development and manufacture of a demonstrator system was awarded to TRW as prime contractor, the deadline for completion being the end of 1997, subsequently extended to March 1998. Despite problems over cost overruns and schedule delays, on 26 June 1999 the first test of the THEL laser took place successfully at TRW's Capistrano test facility in California.

In early 2000, it was announced that tests would be conducted at White Sands in April or May to determine whether THEL could intercept a single Katyusha rocket. If successful, further tests would be carried out against a salvo of rockets. If the tests were successful, the THEL demonstrator would be delivered to Israel. With withdrawal from southern Lebanon scheduled to take place by July and fearing an escalation in Hizbollah attacks on their positions in northern Israel, the Israelis were anxious to deploy THEL as soon as possible and thereafter develop a smaller, mobile version for integration into a missile defence system which would also include the Arrow missile interceptor. In June 2000, it was announced that a test firing of THEL had been carried out, resulting in the successful interception of a rocket.

A further ground-based theatre missile defence system was developed as a concept by the then West German consortium of Diehl and LFK under the auspices of a project commissioned by the Federal Ministry of Defence. Designated the High Energy Laser Experimental (HELEX), it was designed to provide mobile ground-to-air defence against low-level missiles and stand-off weapons launched by aircraft operating from Warsaw Pact bases in neighbouring Poland and Czechoslovakia. The distances from such bases were short and thus any warning times would have been limited. While West Germany already possessed a sophisticated air defence system based on aircraft, missiles and a chain of radar stations, this would have been exposed to heavy electronic countermeasures which would inevitably have degraded its performance. It was considered, however, that a laser air defence system would possibly provide an effective rapid response to any missile threat posed with little warning.

HELEX comprised a multi-megawatt gas dynamic carbon dioxide water-cooled laser, which was powered by burning a liquid consisting of a common hydrocarbon fuel, such as benzene, combined with a nitrogen compound oxidizer. The entire system, including fuel and coolant tanks, was mounted for mobility on a Leopard 2 tracked armoured chassis. Between 5 and 10 tons of laser fuel were carried, this being sufficient for up to approximately fifty shots. In order for the laser projector head and the passive target acquisition system to have a clear line of sight, they were mounted on an elevating arm that enabled them to be raised above surrounding trees or buildings.

Only mirrors suitable for the laser's wavelength of 10,600 nanometers could be used to direct and focus the beam; the use of transmission optics was reportedly excluded due to their fragility. The reflector in the projector head comprised a flexible concave mirror of over 1 metre (3 feet) in diameter. Its shape was altered by a large number of piezoelectric actuators that flexed it to the shape and axial angles needed to produce sufficient concentration of the beam at the required range, while also making the necessary adjustments to compensate for atmospheric turbulence and other factors. The information needed to control the surface of the mirror was furnished by the beam reflected by the target. For the interception of a fast-moving target flying at the speed of sound, the beam would have to be concentrated on the same spot for at least half a second.

HELEX's surveillance and target acquisition system was passive, possibly using satellite monitoring, and thus possessed the advantage of having no signature detectable by enemy electronic surveillance. Furthermore, its survivability in a battlefield environment was enhanced by its mobility, which allowed it to move quickly to a new location if necessary. It was estimated that one HELEX could have controlled an area against incursions by low-level aircraft or missiles up to a range, in good conditions, of nearly 10 kilometres (6 miles) although that figure could have been reduced by up to 50 per cent if the atmosphere in the area was heavily affected by smoke and pollution from battle, that being the principal limitation on the system.

The HELEX project was developed to the point where a small-scale version was tested in trials. It appears, however, that for reasons unknown it was not continued thereafter and was subsequently abandoned.

In addition to intercepting surface-to-surface missiles and rockets, lasers are now being developed for deployment against surface-to-air and air-to-air missiles.

A major threat facing aircraft operating in high risk areas in peacetime, or battlefield environments in time of war, is from man-portable infra-red (IR) guided heat-seeking surface-to-air missiles (SAM) such as the Russian SAM-7 Strela or the American FIM-92A Stinger. During the war in Afghanistan, Mujahideen guerrillas, equipped with Strelas and Stingers, shot down a total of 250 Soviet aircraft in ten years. During the Gulf War of 1991, 80 per cent of US losses of fixed-wing aircraft were reportedly from Iraqi IR-guided SAMs.

Until now, countermeasures against both man-portable SAMs and IR-guided air-to-air missiles have comprised IR decoy systems consisting of flares that are launched to divert missiles from aircraft as they take evasive action. These operate at a temperature higher than that of an aircraft engine and also emit more energy in particular bands of the electromagnetic spectrum. The current generations of IR-guided weapons are, however, equipped with seekers fitted with improved counter-countermeasure (CCM) capabilities, the more advanced types possessing the capability to seek the specific band closest to the heat signature of the aircraft and thus considerably decreasing the effectiveness of IR decoy systems.

Recent years, however, have seen development of systems that will not only provide early warning of attack but also enable aircraft to jam and ultimately destroy missiles. One example is 'Nemesis', formally designated the AN-AAQ-24 Directional Infra-Red Countermeasures (DIRCM). Jointly developed by Britain and the United States, it provides the capability of swift and accurate threat detection, tracking and countermeasures to defeat current and future generation IR-guided missile threats.

Warning systems have long been fitted to fixed-wing aircraft and helicopters to detect the approach of hostile missiles. Early IR-based detection models were, however, far from reliable as they suffered from high levels of false alarm rates. Later systems were designed to search for ultra-violet (UV) signatures that are emitted during missile motor burn. During the early 1980s, the two-colour IR concept assisted in reducing high false alarm rates, the situation being further improved with the development of quadrant UV warning systems. These suffered, however, from 'clutter' caused by UV transmissions from high-powered lighting in such areas as sports stadiums as well as the various types of UV emissions experienced during battlefield conditions. While helicopters are likely to encounter a missile during the period known as 'motor burn', fixed-wing aircraft will more probably be engaged at longer range after power burn-out (PBO), each situation presenting a differing signature in either the ultra-violet or infra-red bands or both.

To overcome such problems, Nemesis is equipped with two missile warning systems (MWS), the AAR-54 UV MWS and AAR-44 IR MWS. The AAR-54 will detect and locate the launch of a missile, tracking it while its rocket motor is burning up until the point of burnout. The AAR-44 thereafter continues to track the weapon in the supersonic, PBO stage of its flight. Each system covers a 90° conical sector while four additional sensors are needed to provide sufficient azimuth and elevation coverage. The MWS will classify potential targets as either clutter, non-threat missiles or hostile missiles and will provide accurate angle of arrival data to the system's fine track sensor (FTS), an imaging IR sensor which, housed in a turret assembly, tracks an incoming threat missile. Large rotary and fixed-wing aircraft, such as the CH-47 Chinook or C-130 Hercules transport, are fitted with turrets on either side of the fuselage. Thus a missile is tracked even through the nadir region and will be handed from jammer to jammer if it crosses into another sector during its homing phase.

Also housed in each turret are two 3-inch infra-red xenon or krypton flash lamps; those on smaller aircraft, such as the Lynx helicopter, are fitted with a single 2-inch lamp. As the missile is being tracked by the FTS, the lamps transmit modulated jamming energy at the missile's homing head, blinding it and causing the missile to drop away. Each turret assembly is also designed for optional installation of an air-cooled diode-pumped IR laser, operating in the mid-band region of the electro-magnetic spectrum which is eye-safe and can be used in populated areas. This will enable the system to cope with any missiles which may in the future be designed to overcome jamming by infra-red lamp systems.

During tests in 1998, the Nemesis DIRCM system proved highly successful. In June, live firing tests were conducted in the United States at the White Sands test range. Twelve IR-guided missiles were launched at an unmanned DIRCM-equipped helicopter, suspended from a cable and towed between two mountain peaks, and the system succeeded in defeating all of them.

At the time of writing, DIRCM is currently in early production and among the first to bring it into service will be the US Air Force Special Operations Command, which will fit sixty systems to its AC-130H/U Spectre gunships and MC-130E/H Combat Talon I/II special operations transports. In addition, a total of 131 systems will reportedly be fitted to fixed and rotary wing aircraft of the Royal Air Force and Royal Navy. A system for fast jets, designated Laser Infra-Red Counter Measures (LIRCM) and fitted only with a laser unit, is currently under development.

The concept of laser defence has recently been extended to countering anti-armour guided missiles by Northrop Grumman which has developed a system that will detect, track and jam such weapons. Designated the Directed Missile Countermeasure Device (DMCD) and designed to be mounted on an armoured vehicle, the system comprises four missile warning systems and a laser emitting 425 watts. It utilizes closed-loop tracking to maintain the laser beam on the missile and smart jamming techniques to maximize distances by which the latter will miss the vehicle. At the same time, it provides accurate data on the position and range of the missile launcher, its four MSWs picking up the signature of the launch. The system itself is fully stabilized so that the beam can be maintained on the missile even while the vehicle is mobile.

Lasers can also be used to detect and neutralize enemy electro-optical systems. One such system, developed for the US Army during the 1990s, was Stingray which was designed to detect and counter optical and electro-optical devices such as thermal imagers and rangefinders. This comprised a low-powered target acquisition laser and a high-powered device designed to neutralize optical and electro-optical targets. Developed for use on the Bradley M2 Infantry Fighting Vehicle, it was intended to enhance the vehicle's survivability on the battlefield. Two prototype systems were deployed on Bradleys in Kuwait during the Gulf War in 1991 but reportedly were not used during combat. A lightweight version of Stingray, designated Outrider, was subsequently developed for the US Marine Corps for mounting on the 0.50 calibre heavy machine-gun mount on the High-Mobility Multi-purpose Wheeled vehicle, popularly known as the 'Hummer'. Neither system, however, progressed beyond prototype stage and both development programmes were ultimately terminated.

The mid-1990s saw the development of man-portable laser systems for target acquisition and designation purposes with small arms and other weapons systems. Among these is the Target Location and Observation System (TLOS), a lightweight image-intensified day/night sight system using a low-powered infra-red laser to acquire direct-view electro-optical targets. Designed for use with either individual or crew-served weapons, the system comprises a laser projector, a third-generation image intensifier and two field-of-view objective lenses, and is capable of target acquisition and designation as well as night observation tasks. Weighing nearly 4.5 kilograms (9³/₄ pounds), TLOS has a detection range of 3,000 metres (9,840 feet) at night and 2,000 metres (6,560 feet) during the day.

Lasers have also featured in the development of non-lethal weapons. One such device is the SABER 203 which was developed by the Phillips Laboratory at Kirtland. Configured to the same shape and dimensions as a 40-mm grenade round and designed for use in the M203 launcher fitted under the barrel of the M16A2 rifle, the low-power device projected a beam intended to dazzle and disorientate a person. A number of SABER 203s were deployed with US Marine Corps units during Operation Restore Hope, which took place in Somalia from December 1992 to mid-1994, and it was found that when beams were projected on to torsos rather than into eyes, as the device had not been declared eye-safe, it had a dramatic effect on Somali gunmen who panicked and ran. Consequently, further development of the concept as a non-lethal weapon system was carried out under the name Hindering Adversaries with Less-than-lethal Technology (HALT) and the result was a device which can be mounted on an M-16 rifle or M4 carbine, with a hand-held version being planned for the future. In effect the device, which is eye-safe at point of emission from the projector, serves as a warning to belligerents, showing them that they are in the aiming point of a weapon and could be subject to lethal force if they persist in showing aggression.

The use of lasers for blinding is not permitted under the terms of the 1980 Certain Conventional Weapons Convention (CCWC), to which the United States and Russia are signatories. Its Amended Protocol IV, prohibits the use or transfer of laser weapons specifically designed to cause permanent blindness to unenhanced vision (the naked eye or the eye with corrective lenses). However, the potential of even low-powered lasers to cause long-lasting damage to vision or blindness is considerable. Aircrews have proved particularly susceptible to this threat, as was illustrated by an incident which took place in the United States on 4 April 1997. On that date, a Canadian Armed Forces CH-124 helicopter was tasked with carrying out surveillance on a Russian merchant vessel, the *Kapitan Man*, which was tracking a US Navy strategic ballistic missile submarine (SSBN), the USS *Ohio*, which was based at the US naval base at Bremerton in the state of Washington.

Aboard the aircraft, in addition to the pilot Captain Patrick Barnes, was Lieutenant Jack Daly, an officer of the Office of Naval Intelligence (ONI) serving at the Canadian Pacific Maritime Forces Command at Esquimalt, on Vancouver Island in the state of Victoria, as a member of the ONI's Foreign Intelligence Liaison Officer (FILO) Program. The role of the Program was to monitor the movements and activities of the *Kapitan Man* and a number of other spy ships, one Russian and others sailing under Chinese, Cypriot and Panamanian flags, which monitored the movements of nine US SSBNs operating out of their base at Bremerton. Four years previously, the *Kapitan Man* had been searched by the US authorities and was found to have anti-submarine warfare equipment on board; a subsequent search uncovered the presence of sonobuoys.

When the helicopter caught up with the *Kapitan Man*, she was one of three vessels in the Strait of Juan de Fuca, 8 kilometres (5 miles) north of the Port of Los Angeles, heading towards Puget Sound. The aircraft circled three times before passing over the ship, during which time Lieutenant Daly filmed it with a digital camera. While doing so, however, he was unaware that he was being 'lased' – attacked with a laser. On returning to Esquimalt, his camera was handed over to another member of the US Navy intelligence staff for downloading of the images, which clearly showed a red dot of bright light on the bridge of the *Kapitan Man*. By that time, Lieutenant Daly was suffering from a severe headache and irritation to his right eye. On the following day he was experiencing severe pain and discomfort, and examination of the eye revealed that the eyeball was swollen. That night Captain Barnes began to suffer similar problems.

A subsequent medical examination of Lieutenant Daly's right eye revealed four or five lesions on the retina, caused, specialists believed, by a 'repetitive pulsed laser'. While Captain Barnes appeared to be less injured, possibly because his helmet visor was lowered at the time, his eyes were also permanently damaged. Both men subsequently suffered constant pain and deteriorating vision. As a result of his injuries, Captain Barnes was grounded after the incident and told that he would never fly again.

As for the *Kapitan Man*, she was subsequently boarded by the US Coast Guard but the Russian crew refused to allow certain areas of the vessel to be searched. According to an article by journalist Bill Gertz, published in the *Washington Post*, the Russian embassy had been warned of the search beforehand by the State Department, giving time for the laser to be concealed. It appeared that the Clinton administration was prepared to allow the Russians to get away with committing a hostile act in order to avoid jeopardizing relations with them.

Another laser attack on aircrew took place on 24 October 1998 during peacekeeping missions in Bosnia near the town of Zenica, when the pilot and a crew member of a UH-60 Blackhawk helicopter came under attack from a laser on the ground. Both suffered minor burns to their corneas and had to be removed temporarily from flying duty. There were suspicions that the attack was carried out with a small hand-held device but such was the threat posed that US helicopter aircrews were thereafter issued with special protective glasses.

Similar incidents have also occurred in the United States, commercial airline crews being temporarily incapacitated by lasers. The pilot and co-pilot of a Boeing 737 taking off from Los Angeles were hit by a burst from a laser that lasted between five and ten seconds; the co-pilot suffering burns to his right eye and broken blood vessels. In another incident, a member of the crew of an aircraft landing at Phoenix, Arizona, was blinded by a laser, suffering after-images and loss of night vision for about one and a half hours afterwards. In November 1998, the National Air Intelligence Centre reported that lasers had been responsible for over fifty incidents of blinding of aircrew in the United States alone.

Lasers are seen by many as the weapons of the future. Proponents of the technology emphasize in particular their non-lethal potential in being able to disarm an enemy with minimum collateral damage and loss of life, able to be calibrated to cause either minimum damage or totally destroy targets far more precisely than conventional weapons. Furthermore, they have much to offer as defensive systems, from shooting down ballistic missiles to defeating SAMs targeted on aircraft or anti-armour guided weapons launched at armoured vehicles. Without a doubt, lasers will before long form an essential part of any modern arsenal.

TIMELINE

The following chronology shows the specifications of the key weapons that entered service between 1944 and 1990.

Entered Service	Country of Origin	Type	Designation	Warhead	Range
1944	Germany	Cruise	V1	900 kg (1,980 lb) high explosive	240 kms (5,000 miles)
1944	Germany	SRBM	V2	750 kg (1,600 lb) high explosive	320 kms (200 miles)
1954	USA	Rocket	MGR-1 Honest John	2, 20 or 40 kilotons	19 kms (12 miles)
1958	USSR	SLBM	SS-N-4 Sark	1.2–2 megatons	560 kms (350 miles)
1960	USA	SLBM	Polaris A-1	1 megaton	2,200 kms (1,400 miles)
1961	USSR	IRBM	SS-5 Skean	1 megaton	3,700 kms (2,300 miles)
1961	USA	ICBM	Titan I	4 megatons	8,000 kms (5,000 miles)
1961	USA	SLBM	Polaris A-2	3×200 kilotons	2,800 kms (1,750 miles)
1962	USA	ICBM	Minuteman I	1 megaton	8,000 kms (5,000 miles)
1962	USA	IRBM	MGM-31 Pershing 1a	400 kilotons	740 kms (460 miles)
1963	USSR	ICBM	SS-8 Sasin	5 megatons	11,260 kms (7,200 miles)
1963	USA	ICBM	Titan II	9 megatons	8,000 kms (5,000 miles)
1964	USA	SLBM	Polaris A-3	3×60 kiloton MIRV	4,720 kms (2,950 miles)
1965	USSR	ICBM	SS-9 Scarp	3×5 megaton MRV or 1×20–25 megaton	12,000 kms (7,500 miles)
1965	USA	ICBM	Minuteman II	1.2 megaton	13,000 kms (8,000 miles)
1965	USSR	Rocket	FROG-7	200 kilotons	65 kms (105 miles)

Entered Service	Country of Origin	Type	Designation	Warhead	Range
1965	USSR	SRBM	SS-1C Scud B	1 megaton	180 kms (110 miles)
1968	USSR	SLBM	SS-N-6 Sawfly	1 megaton	3,000 kms (1,860 miles)
1969	USSR	SRBM	SS-12 Scaleboard	500 kilotons	700–800 kms (435–500 miles)
1970	USA	ICBM	Minuteman III	3×170 kiloton MIRV	9,650 kms (6,000 miles)
1971	USA	SLBM	Poseidon C-3	10–14 40 kiloton MIRV	4,000–5,200 kms (2,485–3,230 miles)
1971	USA	SRBM	MGM-52 Lance	100 kilotons	120 kms (75 miles)
1976	USSR	IRBM	SS-20 Model 1	1 megaton	2,750 kms (1,700 miles)
1976	USSR	SLBM	SS-N-18 Model 1 Stingray	7×150 kiloton MIRV	6,500 kms (4,000 miles)
1978	USSR	SRBM	SS-21 Spider	100 kilotons	120 kms (75 miles)
1978	USSR	ICBM	SS-18 Satan (Model 2)	8×600 kilotons 1.6 megatons	9,250 kms (5,750 miles)
1979	USA	SLBM	Trident I C4	8×100 kilotons	6,800 kms (4,200 miles)
1984	USA	IRBM	Pershing II	5–50 kilotons	1,800 kms (1,120 miles)
1984	USSR	SLBM	SS-N-20 Sturgeon	10×100 kilotons	8,300 kms (5,160 miles)
1985	USSR	SRBM	SS-23 Scarab	200 kilotons	500 kms (310 miles)
1989	USA	SLBM	Trident II D5	8 or 14×375 kilotons	7,400–11,100 kms (4,560–6,900 miles)

GLOSSARY
of abbreviations

A&E	Audits and Examinations
ABL	Airborne Laser
ABM	Anti-Ballistic Missile Systems
AERE	Atomic Energy Research Establishment
AFSA	Armed Forces Security Agency
ALL	Airborne Laser Laboratory
AMEC	Arctic Military Environmental Co-operation
AP	Armour-piercing ammunition
APFSDS-T	Armour-piercing Fin-stabilized Discarding Sabot Tracer
ATACMS	Army Tactical Missile System
ATAS	Air-to-Air Stinger
ATL	Airborne Tactical Laser
AWACS	Airborne Warning and Control System
BAT	Brilliant Anti-Tank
BILL	Beacon Illuminator Laser
BKA	Federal Criminal Bureau
BMDO	Ballistic Missile Defence Organization
BND	German intelligence service (Bundesnachtrichtendienst)
C3I	Command, Control, Communications and Intelligence
CCM	Counter-Counter Measure
CCWC	Certain Conventional Weapons Convention
CEP	Circular Error Probability
CIA	Central Intelligence Agency
CISCO	Commonwealth of Independent States Co-operation
COIL	Chemical Oxygen Iodine Laser
CTR	Co-operative Threat Reduction (*aka* Nunn-Lugar) Program
DATEN	Department of Atomic Energy
DIRCM	Directional Infra-Red Counter Measures
DMCD	Directed Missile Countermeasure Device
DSMAC	Digital Scene Matching Area Correlator
DVO	Direct View Optic sight unit

FBI	Federal Bureau of Investigation
FCR	Fire Control Radar
FILO	Foreign Intelligence Liaison Officer
FLIR	Forward-looking Infra-red System
FTS	Fine Track Sensor
GAN	Russian State Nuclear Regulator
GCS	Ground Control Station
GMLRS	Guided Multi-Launch Rocket Systems
GPS	Global Positioning System
GRU	Main Intelligence Directorate of the General Staff
GSM	Ground Station Module
HA	Heavy Armour
HALT	Hindering Adversaries with Less-than-lethal Technology
HE	High Explosive ammunition
HEAT	High Explosive Anti-Tank ammunition
HEAT-MP-T	High Explosive Anti-Tank Multi-Purpose Tracer
HEDP	High Explosive Dual Purpose ammunition
HEI	High Explosive Incendiary ammunition
HELEX	High Energy Laser Experimental
HESH	High Explosive Squash Head ammunition
ICBM	Intercontinental Ballistic Missiles
IFF	Identification Friend or Foe
IHADSS	Integrated Helmet and Display Sighting System
INF	Intermediate-Range Nuclear Forces Treaty
IR	Infra-Red
IRBM	Intermediate Range Ballistic Missiles
IRST	Infra-Red Search and Track
JSTARS	Joint Surveillance Target Attack Radar System
KGB	Soviet security police
LANTIRN	Low Altitude Navigation and Targeting Infra-Red for Night
LIRCM	Laser Infra-Red Counter Measures
LKA	Bavaria's State Criminal Bureau
LRF/D	Laser Rangefinder/Designator
MAD	Mutual Assured Destruction
MADM	Medium Atomic Demolition Munitions
MaRV	Manoeuvring warhead

MBT	Main Battle Tanks
MCS	Master Control Station
Minatom	Russian Ministry of Nuclear Energy
MIRACL	Mid-Infra-Red Advanced Chemical Laser
MIRV	Multiple Independently Targeted Re-entry Vehicles
MLRS	Multi-Rocket Launch Rocket System
MOX	Mixed Uranium-plutonium Dioxide
MPC&A	Material Protection, Control and Accounting Program
MRBM	Medium Range Ballistic Missiles
MRV	Multiple Re-entry Vehicles
MWS	Missile Warning System
NASA	US National Aeronautical and Space Administration
NATO	North Atlantic Treaty Organisation
NBC	Nuclear Biological and Chemical warfare
NKVD	Soviet secret police
NSA	National Security Agency
ONI	Office of Naval Intelligence
PBO	Post-Burnout
PDRR	Program Definition and Risk Reduction
PNVS	Pilot Night Vision Sensor
PPS	Precise Positioning Service Programme
RAAF	Royal Australian Air Force
RAF	Royal Air Force
RAN	Royal Australian Navy
RARDE	Royal Armaments Research and Development Establishment
RFI	Radio Frequency Interferometer
RPVs/UAVs	Remotely Piloted Vehicles
RSTA	Reconnaissance, Surveillance and Target Acquisition
RVSN	Strategic Rocket Forces (Raketnyye Voyska Strategicheskogo Naznacheniya)
SADM	Special Atomic Demolition Munitions
SALT	Strategic Arms Limitation Talks
SAM	Surface-to-Air missile
SBL	Space-Borne Lasers
SCDL	Surveillance Control Data Link
SCS	Scientific Civil Service

SDI	Strategic Defence Initiative
SDIO	Strategic Defence Initiative Organization
SEAD	Suppression of Enemy Air Defences aircraft
SEP	System Enhancement Programme
SIS	Secret Intelligence Service
SLBM	Submarine-Launched Ballistic Missiles
SMDC	Space and Missile Defence Command
SPS	Standard Positioning Service
SRBM	Short Range Ballistic Missiles
SSBN	Strategic Ballistic Missile Submarines
START	Strategic Arms Reductions Talks
SVR	External Intelligence Agency (Sluzhba Vneshney Razvedki)
TADS	Target Acquisition Designation Sights system
TBM	Theatre Ballistic Missiles
TCU	Tracking Communication Unit
THEL	Tactical High Energy Laser
TI	Infra-Red Thermal Imager
TIALD	Thermal Imaging Airborne Laser Designator
TILL	Tracking Illuminator Laser
TLOS	Target Location and Observation System
TOW	Tube-launched, Optically-tracked, Wire-guided missile
TV	Television
UN	United Nations
USAF	United States Air Force
UV	Ultra-Violet

SELECTED BIBLIOGRAPHY

Andrew, Christopher and Vasili Mitrokhin. *The Mitrokhin Archive – The KGB in Europe and The West.* Allen Lane, London 1999.

Arnold, Lorna. *A Very Special Relationship – British Atomic Weapon Trials in Australia.* Her Majesty's Stationery Office, London 1987.

Bishop, Chris (ed.). *The Directory of Modern Military Weapons.* Greenwich Editions, London 1999.

Bonds, Ray (ed.) *The Soviet War Machine – An Encyclopedia of Russian Military Equipment and Strategy.* Salamander, London 1976.

Brooks, Geoffrey. *Hitler's Nuclear Weapons.* Leo Cooper, London 1992.

Bunn, Matthew. *The Next Wave – Urgently Needed New Steps to Control Warheads and Fissile Material.* Carnegie Endowment for International Peace, Washington 2000.

Clancy, Tom with General Chuck Horner. *Every Man a Tiger.* Sidgwick & Jackson, London 2000.

Cockburn, Andrew & Leslie. *One Point Safe – The Terrifying Threat of Russia's Unwanted Nuclear Arsenal.* Little Brown, London 1997.

Darwish, Adel & Gregory Alexander. *Unholy Babylon – The Secret History of Saddam's War.* Victor Gollancz, London 1991.

Dorril, Stephen. *MI6 – Fifty Years of Special Operations.* Fourth Estate, London 2000.

Gowing, Margaret. *Britain And Atomic Energy 1939–1945.* Macmillan, London 1964.

Shields, John M. & William C. Potter. *Dismantling the Cold War – US and NIS Perspectives on the Nunn-Lugar Cooperative Threat Reduction Program.* MIT Press, Cambridge, Mass. 1997.

Young, Peter. *The Machinery of War – An Illustrated History of Weapons.* Hart-Davis MacGibbon, London 1973.

INDEX

Blackjack 94
Blair, Bruce 126–7
Bock's Car 77
Boeing 208, 209
Bradley M2 Infantry Fighting
Vehicle 181–3, 221
Bradley M3 Cavalry Fighting
Vehicle 182
Brezhnev, Leonid 82
*The Bulletin of the Atomic
Scientists* 143
Bunn, Matthew 138, 149
Bush, Dr Vannnevar 33
Bushehr project 147–8
Bush, George 92
Butement, W. A. S. 67
Bykov, Colonel Robert 124–5,
126, 127

C
Cairncross, John 29
cannons 13
Carter, President Jimmy 82
1980 Certain Conventional
Weapons Convention 222–3
Chadwick, Professor James 27, 34
Challenger 1 174–5
Challenger 2 175–6
Challens, John 45–6, 69, 70–1
Chegets 112, 117–18, 120
chemical oxygen iodine laser
(COIL) 207, 212
chemical weapons 93, 162
1993 Chemical Weapons
Convention 93
Cheshire, Group Captain
Leonard 43
Churchill, Winston 30, 32, 33,
34, 60
circular error probability (CEP)
158
Clinton, President Bill 92, 148,
214, 224
Cockburn, Andrew 141, 148
Cockburn, Leslie 141, 148
Cockcroft, Professor John
37–8, 41

codebreaking 53–4
Cold War 17, 73, 91–2, 111, 114,
116, 121, 128
Colt, Samuel 14
Commonwealth of Independent
States Co-operation
Programme (CISCO) 108
Condor-2 160–1
Co-operative Threat
Reduction (CTR) Program
21–2, 92–8, 107, 109,
110, 121, 146
Corner, John 46
Cosmos-2224 115
counter-countermeasures (CCM)
218
Crécy, Battle of 12
cruise missiles 23, 85–6, 94,
154–5, 157

D
Daily Telegraph 99
Dale, Geoffrey 46
Daly, Lieutenant Jack 223–4
Dark Ages 12
Davy Crockett tactical nuclear
weapon 128–9
Defend America Act 205
de la Billière, General Sir Peter
195
Denisov, Vladimir 130, 133
Deptula, Lieutenant Colonel
David 156
Deutch, John 138
Digital Scene Matching Area
Correlator (DSMAC) 157
Directed Infra-red
Countermeasures (DIRCM)
218, 220
Directed Missile Countermeasure
Device (DMCD) 220
dumb bombs 158

E
E-3 Sentry AWACS 167–9
Einstein, Albert 39, 73–4
Enola Gay 76